THE STORY OF THE

JUBILEE SINGERS;

WITH THEIR SONGS

AMS PRESS

NEW YORK

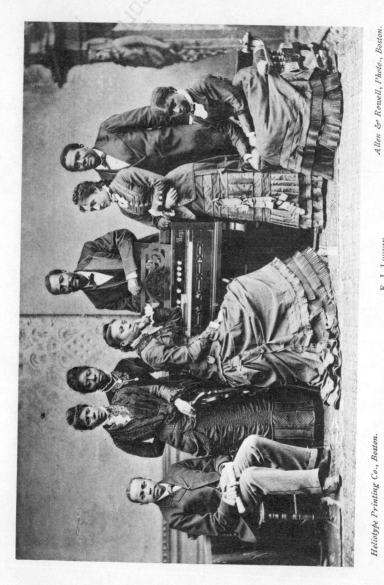

F. J. LOUDIN.

MAGGIE L. PORTER.   JENNIE JACKSON.   MABEL R. LEWIS.   R. A. HALL.

GEORGE E. BARRETT   ELLA SHEPARD   PATTI MALONE.

THE STORY OF THE
JUBILEE SINGERS;

WITH THEIR SONGS.

BY

J. B. T. MARSH.

Revised Edition.

FIFTY-NINTH THOUSAND.

BOSTON:
HOUGHTON, OSGOOD AND COMPANY.
The Riverside Press, Cambridge.
1880.

Reprinted from the edition of 1880, Boston
First AMS EDITION published 1971
Manufactured in the United States of America

International Standard Book Number: 0-404-04189-2
Library of Congress Catalog Number: 72-165509

AMS PRESS INC.
NEW YORK, N.Y. 10003

NOTE.

———•———

THIS volume is in part an abridgment of the two Jubilee Histories which were written by the Rev. G. D. Pike, and which have had a wide circulation, one giving an account of the first campaign in America, and the other of the first visit to Great Britain. But the interval between these two narratives is here bridged over, and the story is brought down to the return of the Jubilee Singers from Germany.

The personal histories have been more fully written out, and a large number of new songs have been added, including several of the most popular pieces ever given in the Jubilee concerts.

J. B. T. M.

CONTENTS.

CHAPTER I.

THE YEAR OF JUBILEE.

CHAPTER II.

THE FORLORN HOPE.

CHAPTER III.

ADRIFT ON STORMY SEAS.

CHAPTER IV.

LIGHT IN THE EAST.

CHAPTER V.

SUCCESS AT LAST.

CHAPTER VI.

THE SECOND CAMPAIGN.

CHAPTER VII.

THE FIRST VISIT TO LONDON.

CHAPTER XI.

PERSONAL HISTORIES OF THE SINGERS.

THE STORY

OF THE

JUBILEE SINGERS.

———◆———

CHAPTER I.

THE YEAR OF JUBILEE.

THE story of the Jubilee Singers seems almost as little like a chapter from real life as the legend of the daring Argonauts who sailed with Jason on that famous voyage after the Golden Fleece. It is the story of a little company of emancipated slaves who set out to secure, by their singing, the fabulous sum of $20,000 for the impoverished and unknown school in which they were students. The world was as unfamiliar to these untraveled freed people as were the countries through which the Argonauts had to pass; the social prejudices that confronted them were as terrible to meet as fire-breathing bulls or the warriors that sprang from the land sown with dragons' teeth; and no seas were ever more tempestuous than the stormy experiences that for a time tested their faith and courage.

They were at times without the money to buy needed clothing. Yet in less than three years they returned, bringing back with them nearly one hundred thousand dollars. They had been turned away from hotels, and driven out of railway waiting-rooms, because of their color. But they had been received with honor by the President of the United States, they had sung their slave-songs before the Queen of Great Britain, and they had gathered as invited guests about the breakfast-table of her Prime Minister. Their success was as remarkable as their mission was unique.

The civil war which broke out in the United States, in 1861, was avowedly waged, on one side to overthrow the Union of the States, and on the other to preserve it. But back of this object it was really a war, on one side to perpetuate slavery, and on the other to abolish it. The South understood this from the start. So did those at the North who were wise to read the signs of the times, and especially those who had the spiritual instinct to interpret the meaning of God's providences.

The anti-slavery reformers, who had sought, through the peaceful agencies of the press, the pulpit, and the platform, to secure the abolition of slavery, went into the war with an ardor they never could have felt in the struggle of a slave-holding nation for mere political existence. No young men responded to the call for troops more heartily than those whose boyhood homes had been stations on the Underground Railway — that unique line whose stock was never offered in market; whose trains ran only by night; whose tracks were country by-roads; whose coaches were plain farm wagons; whose pas-

sengers were fugitive slaves; whose terminus was
the free soil of Canada. The first detachment of
Union troops that passed through Baltimore on its
way to Washington made the streets of that sullen
city ring with a song in honor of old John Brown,
the abolitionist of Harper's Ferry. And regiment
after regiment of volunteers, the pride and flower of
half a million Northern homes, "rallied round the
flag, shouting the battle-cry of freedom."

The slaves, too, utterly ignorant as they were of
common political issues and the proportions of the
struggle, almost everywhere and at once read the
significance of the great conflict. Tidings of every
turn in the fortunes of war passed from cabin to
cabin by some mysterious telegraphy, and every
Union victory was the signal for secret thanksgiving
services.

It was the natural result that the camps of the
Union army should at once become cities of refuge
for fugitive slaves. A New England general, who
had been in close political alliance with the slave
power until it raised its hand to strike down the
Union, gave them a name and a recognized standing
in the military lines as "contraband of war." And
by and by there came from the good President who
had so patiently bided the time, the proclamation
that made the army, in the aim as well as the incident of its work, an army of emancipation.

Its advance was the signal for a rally of slaves
from all the country round to follow it, they knew
not whither, save that it was to freedom. They
flocked in upon the line of march by bridle-paths
and across the fields; old men on crutches, babies

on their mothers' backs ; women wearing the cast-off
blue jackets of Yankee cavalry-men, boys in abbre-
viated trousers of rebel gray ; sometimes lugging
a bundle of household goods snatched from their
cabins as they fled, sometimes riding an old mule
"borrowed" from "mas'r," but oftener altogether
empty-handed, with nothing whatever to show for
their life-time of unrewarded toil.   But they were
free ; and with what swinging of ragged hats, and
tumult of rejoicing hearts and fervent "God bless
you's," they greeted their deliverers !   "The year of
jubilee," of which they had sung and for which they
had prayed and waited so many years, had come at
last !

By this violent emancipation of war — so different
in its process from the peaceful abolition for which
the friends of the slave had been so long looking
and laboring — over four millions of bondmen were
suddenly made free.   They were homeless, penni-
less, ignorant, improvident — unprepared in every
way for the 'dangers as well as the duties of freedom.   Self-reliance they had · never had the opportunity to learn, and, suddenly left to shift for themselves, they were at the mercy of the knaves who
were everywhere so ready to cheat them out of their
honest earnings.   They had been kept all their lives
in a school of immorality, and even church member-
ship was no evidence that one was not a thief, a liar,
or a libertine.   Their former masters were so im-
poverished by their emancipation, along with the
other costs of the war, that they had little ability —
and were so exasperated by it that they had usually
still less disposition — to help them.

The task of giving these freed slaves a Christian education was laid mainly, therefore, upon the Christian people of the North. It was a missionary work of such magnitude and character as no people was ever called to take up before. Schools were started — even before the close of the first six months of the war — in little cabins, in army tents, in unfloored log chapels, in abandoned slave marts, under the open sky. Hundreds of Northern ladies, many of them from homes of luxury and culture, came to teach these degraded people the A B C's of the spelling-book and of Christian citizenship.

The work was full of discomforts, difficulties, and danger. By the varying fortunes of war the schools were often broken up, and the teachers forced to seek safety for their lives in flight. Overworked, unable sometimes to obtain suitable food, shelter, or medical attendance, many of these brave women laid down their lives in the cause, as truly as a soldier who is buried on the field of battle. Even after the war they were shunned as lepers in Southern society, and more than one teacher was assassinated by the Ku Klux banditti for refusing to obey their anonymous warnings to give up the work and leave the State.

But their mission was not without its brighter side. God's Spirit was often present with converting power in the schools, and in the prayer-meetings that always went hand-in-hand with the schools. All their lives, the lash or the auction-block had been the swift penalty for slaves who were caught learning to read. Now that the fetters had fallen from mind as well as body there came an eagerness to learn that was like a consuming fire. The world never saw such a sight before as these schools presented.

Families pinched with hunger asked more eagerly for schools than for bread. Women of threescore and ten sometimes mastered the alphabet in a week. Old men bent over the same spelling-books with their grandchildren. Fathers would work all day to support their families, and walk every night to an evening school miles away. Girls suspended from school privileges for a few days, for some wrong-doing, would plead instead for the penalty of a whipping. Their gratitude for instruction was as fervent as their desire for it was ravenous, and their attachment to their teachers was most devoted.

The first school for the freedmen was started by teachers sent out for that purpose by the American Missionary Association. This society was formed in 1846, because of the acquiescent attitude towards slavery of most of the older missionary organizations. It had sustained missions among the negroes of Jamaica and West Africa. Its home missionaries in the slave-holding States, while striving to reach both white and black with schools and the preaching of the gospel, had always faithfully borne testimony against the great sin of slavery. It had the confidence and support of the friends of freedom. And when this great task of giving more than four millions of freedmen a Christian education was suddenly laid upon the nation, its origin, its associations, and its past labors, all pointed to it as providentially trained up for the occasion. And to it a large part of the work has fallen.

In 1863 it had 83 ministers and teachers in this field; in 1864, 250; in 1868, 532. Since the work began it has expended about $3,000,000 in it. As public schools came to be opened, to some extent, for the colored people, and as the importance of permanent institutions for the training of teachers and ministers from among the freedmen themselves became more apparent, and the necessity for them more imperative, the Association withdrew for the most part from this temporary primary work, and concentrated its efforts upon a system of training-schools.

Besides the seventeen academies and normal schools which it has planted at central points throughout the South, and which require the services of nearly a hundred skilled teachers, it has under its fostering care seven chartered institutions for collegiate and theological education. These are located in as many different States, and no two of them are within three hundred miles of each other. They are Berea College, at Berea, Kentucky; Hampton Institute, at Hampton, Virginia; Fisk University, at Nashville, Tennessee; Atlanta University, at Atlanta, Georgia; Talladega College, at Talladega, Alabama; Tougaloo University, at Tougaloo, Mississippi; and Straight University, at New Orleans, Louisiana.

CHAPTER II.

THE FORLORN HOPE.

THE first steps towards the establishment òf Fisk University were taken in the autumn of 1865. Rev. E. P. Smith, after rendering invaluable service to the Union army during the war as the Field Agent of the United States Christian Commission, had just taken up the work of Secretary of the American Missionary Association at Cincinnati. Rev. E. M. Cravath, early in the war, had exchanged the ministrations of an Ohio parish for those of an army chaplaincy. The son of a pioneer Abolitionist, whose home was a busy station on the "Underground Railway," and whose children were thus inoculated from their earliest days with anti-slavery convictions and a special interest in the colored race, his army experience had brought him into such acquaintance with the needs of the Freedmen, that, at the close of the war, he was commissioned by the Association for special service in organizing its schools in the same department to which Mr. Smith had been assigned.

These two met at Nashville. Carefully surveying the field, they were convinced that this was a central point where a permanent university ought to be planted for the higher education of the freed people, to equip their ministers and teachers, and to give

their leaders in all departments of the life now open
ing before them a Christian training for their work.

As the capital city of Tennessee, and as the base
of some of the most extensive and decisive military
operations of the war, Nashville was not only a point
of great business, social, and political importance,
but the centre of a large colored population. Eight
of the thirteen formerly slave-holding States sur-
round and actually border upon Tennessee, and in
it and them four fifths of the freed people have their
homes.

To aid in starting such an important enterprise,
there were, providentially, two other efficient friends
of the freed people at hand, — General Clinton B.
Fisk, the distinguished Christian soldier then in
charge of the Freedmen's Bureau in the District of
Kentucky and Tennessee; and Professor John Ogden, formerly Principal of the Minnesota State Normal School, and afterwards an officer in the Union
army, but at that time resident in Nashville as the
agent of the Western Freedmen's Aid Commission,
— a society which was afterwards merged into the
American Missionary Association.

These four took hold of the work, but were met at
the outset by two formidable difficulties. A site and
buildings of its own were absolutely essential to the
success of the undertaking. The Association at that
time had no funds that it felt at liberty to invest in
real estate for such an enterprise. More than that,
the dominant element in the community was so hos-
tile to any effort to elevate the colored people, that
it was next to impossible to purchase land for such
uses. But a favorable site was found and secured,

without the purpose for which it was wanted being made known to the seller ; three of these friends of the work becoming individually responsible for the entire purchase-money of $16,000.

One of the chief advantages of the location was the fact that it was already occupied by a group of one-story frame buildings, which had been erected and used for hospital barracks by the Union army. It was known that these could be obtained from the government, and be easily and cheaply adapted to the present necessities of the enterprise.   And so, in January, 1866, the new school was opened.   The occasion was the most notable event of the sort in the history of the colored people of Tennessee.   Governor Brownlow made a short address, and other distinguished gentlemen in civil and military life were present.   There was inspiration for the freed people in the very thought of thus founding a university for the emancipated slaves, who had all their life long been forbidden the slightest knowledge of letters.

The officers' quarters became the home of an earnest band of teachers ; the sick-wards were fitted up as school-rooms, and filled with hundreds of eager children ; the dead-house was turned into a store-room of supplies for the naked and hungry.   And there was an almost pathetic romance in the work when a pile of rusty handcuffs and fetters from the abandoned slave-pen of the city came into the possession of the school, and were sold as old iron, and the money invested in the purchase of Testaments and spelling-books !

The number of pupils in daily attendance the first

year averaged over one thousand. Some who began the first term never ceased attendance until they had graduated, ten years afterwards, from a full collegiate course. At first the instruction was, of necessity, of an elementary sort. But the idea upon which the school was avowedly founded, of providing the highest collegiate advantages, was kept prominently in view. In 1867 the action of the city of Nashville, in making some provision for public schools at which colored children could be educated, relieved the school of many of its primary pupils and opened the way for more perfectly carrying out the original purpose. A university charter was obtained. Some of the buildings which had been used as schoolrooms were refitted as dormitories, into which students from abroad, eager for a higher education, at once began to gather. It was not long before the number applying for admission was greater than could be accommodated.

There never was a hive of busier workers. As they became qualified for the work, the students went out to teach, — missionaries to lift up their less-favored fellows. Many of them in this way earned the money that enabled them to return again and go on farther with their own studies. In a single year as many as 10,000 children have been enrolled in the schools taught by teachers sent out from Fisk, — teachers, some of whom a little while before did not themselves know one letter from another ! The school was pervaded, too, by a religious earnestness that was contagious. The conversion of new students was confidently looked for, and more earnestly sought than their progress in letters.

But along with all this success there had been a steadily increasing occasion of anxiety. The buildings, cheaply and hastily constructed, as they were, for temporary uses, were falling into decay. The site, which had been admirably adapted for the earlier work of the Institution, was found unsuited to its permanent uses. Year by year the problem of obtaining funds for a new site and new buildings grew more and more perplexing. The necessity for its solution at last became imperative, and the University treasurer, Mr. George L. White, undertook to work it out.

Mr. White was a native of Cadiz, New York, born in 1838. A village blacksmith's boy, his school privileges were limited to what he learned in the public school before the age of fourteen. Like so many other Yankee boys while waiting for their work, — or while getting ready for it, — he became a school-teacher. He had inherited from his father a special love for music, and though he had never had any musical instruction himself, and made no pretensions as a vocalist, his schools were famous for the good singing which he had the knack of getting out of his pupils.

Leaving the school-room for the camp, he fought for the Union in the bloody battles of Gettysburg and Chancellorsville ; and the close of the war found him in the employ of the Freedmen's Bureau at Nashville. He had been actively interested in Sunday-school work among the freedmen, and at the opening of Fisk School was invited by Professor Ogden, its principal, to devote his leisure hours to the instruction of the pupils in vocal music. When

Fisk University was chartered he became its treasurer — in other words, its man-of-all-work in business matters.

The progress made by his large singing classes
was a surprise and delight to him. With a presenti-
ment, seemingly, of what was coming, he began to
pick out the most promising voices and give them
that special training for which his own remarkable
range of voice, instinct for musical effect, and magnetism as a drill-master so well fitted him.

In the spring of 1867 he gave a public concert
with his school chorus, which was a great success
financially, and a greater one in opening the eyes of
the white people to the possibilities that lay hidden
in the education of the blacks. A leading daily
interpreted the concert as evidence that the negro
was susceptible of education, and raised the question
whether it was not the duty of the Southern people
to take hold of the work, instead of leaving it to
Northern people with so many radical bees in their
bonnets !

In 1868 he gave another and better concert ; and
in 1870 his now well-drilled classes rendered the
beautiful cantata of "Esther" before a large and
delighted assembly. Taking a part of his choir to
Memphis, he gave a concert to an audience that
filled the opera-house ; and another trip southward
to Chattanooga met with equal success.

About this time the National Teachers' Association of the United States held its annual convention
in Nashville, and arrangements were made for the
Fisk choir to sing in the opening exercises, to the
great disgust of some who were profanely indignant

that "the —— niggers could not be kept in their own places." Other musicians were to favor the convention with their services at the subsequent meetings ; but the singing of the " niggers " proved to be so popular that they were in demand for every session until the close of the convention.

All this while the thought had been taking firmer hold of Mr. White's mind that a student choir might be organized, which could travel through the North and sing out of the people's pocket the money that must soon be obtained in some way for the University. The plan was talked over and prayed over for a year or two. But, turn it to the light in any way they could, the risks seemed too great.

It was one thing to give a paying concert at home, or to make flying trips to points not far away ; it was quite another to start out on a campaign that would certainly involve large expenses, while its returns might be quite inadequate to meet them. Large expenditures would be unavoidable at the start — for the outfit that would be absolutely necessary for these poorly clad students, and for the purchase of their railway tickets to Ohio. The University treasury was almost empty ; the Association did not feel at liberty to risk funds contributed for missionary work in such a speculative venture. And it was not easy to persuade the untraveled parents of some of the students to risk their children in it. But a few clear-headed friends had faith in the plan, and, after much prayer and perplexity of purpose, Mr. White felt the command laid on him from the Lord to go forward.

Taking the little money that was left in the University treasury after buying provisions to last the school for a few days, putting with it all his own, and borrowing on his own notes an amount whose payment, if the venture was a failure, would strip him of every penny of his property, he started out with barely enough money to set his party in working order on the north side of the Ohio River.

CHAPTER III.

THE company as it left Nashville, October 6, 1871, followed by the good wishes, prayers, misgivings, and anxieties of the whole University, numbered thirteen persons. These were Mr. White, who was at the same time the captain, supercargo, pilot, steward, and crew of the ship; Miss Wells, the Principal of an American Missionary Association school at Athens, Alabama, who took the oversight of the girls of the party; and eleven students — Ella Sheppard, Maggie L. Porter, Jennie Jackson, Minnie Tate, Eliza Walker, Phœbe J. Anderson, Thomas Rutling, Benjamin M. Holmes, Greene Evans, Isaac P. Dickerson, and George Wells.

The day after reaching Cincinnati the Singers met with the Rev. Messrs. Halley and Moore, the pastors of the two leading Congregational churches of the city, who were so delighted with their songs that they immediately arranged to hold praise meetings in their churches on Sunday, the next day, that their people might have the pleasure of hearing them. Full audiences greeted them in both services. On Monday a free concert was given and a collection taken at the close. The audience was large but the contribution small.

It was on this Sunday and Monday, so well remembered all over the world, that the great Chicago fire swept away the houses of one hundred thousand people and property to the value of $200,000,000. In Ohio, as everywhere else, people could scarcely think or talk about anything else, much less give money to any other object.

There had not been for ten years a week that would have been, to all appearances, such an unfavorable time for the Singers to commence their work. Out of money and in debt as they were, they donated the entire proceeds of their first paid concert, which amounted to something less than $50, to the Chicago relief fund. This was given in Chillicothe, and called out a card from the Mayor and leading citizens cordially commending to public patronage the two concerts that followed.

Here at Chillicothe they met with an indignity which was often repeated in the next year's experience. Applying at one of the principal hotels for entertainment, they were refused admittance because of their color. Treated in the same way at a second, they only secured shelter at a third by the landlord's giving up his own bedroom to them to use as a parlor, and furnishing them their meals before the usual hour, that his other guests might not leave the house. This odious and cruel caste-spirit it was to be a part of their mission — little as it was in their plans and painful as it was in experience — to break down. It was owing not a little to their triumphant success as singers, and to the story of the distinguished attentions they received from the people of highest rank and culture both

2

in America and Great Britain, that ·the prejudice against color, the hateful heritage of slavery, which was so prevalent and powerful as to make those insults common in their first year's work, was so broken down that they were quite unfrequent in their travels three years afterwards. People who would not sit in the same church-pew with a negro, under the magic of their song were able to get new light on questions of social equality.

Returning to Cincinnati to fill engagements for the Sabbath, they found a dense audience gathered at Mr. Moore's church, in spite of rainy and unpleasant weather. It was hoped that the increasing enthusiasm manifested in connection with these praise services would insure a good audience at the paid concert which had been appointed at Mozart Hall for Tuesday evening; for hotel and traveling bills were already assuming serious proportions. But the receipts were barely sufficient to defray the local expenses of the concert.

However, it was not altogether lost labor. " It was," said one of the dailies, " probably the first concert ever given by a colored troupe in this temple, which has resounded with the notes of the best vocalists of the land. The sweetness of the voices, the accuracy of the execution, and the precision of the time, carried the mind back to the early concerts of the Hutchinsons, the Gibsons, and other famous families, who years ago delighted audiences and taught them with sentiment while they pleased them with melody." Jennie Jackson's rendering of the " Old Folks at Home," as an encore, was received with rapturous applause. Mr. Dickerson sang the "Temperance Medley" here for the first time, and the class trembled for him, as he stood there with his knees beating a tattoo against each other, in a rusty coat that was as much too long for the fashion as his trousers were too short for neighborly acquaintance with his low shoes. But confidence came with the sound of his own voice, and the audience forgot the appearance of the singer in their enjoyment of his song.

Journeying next to Springfield, to fill an appointment for a concert at Black's Opera-house, they found less than twenty people gathered to hear them, and with heavy hearts they announced that they would postpone the entertainment.

A Synod of Presbyterian ministers was in session here, and Mr. White obtained permission for the Singers to appear before them. Assigned a half-hour in which to sing, and state their cause, it was a full hour before the Synod would release them. And not only did they testify their delight " in a vociferous, heartfelt, and decidedly unclerical manner, with hands, feet, and voice," but they passed a resolution "heartily commending them to the favor of the Christian community," and emphasized it by taking up a collection for their benefit of $105.

Working their way in a zig-zag path northward, they gave a concert at Yellow Springs, where the colored Baptist church was kindly placed at their disposal. At Xenia two concerts yielded them $84, and afforded the colored students of Wilberforce University a stimulus that was worth, in another way, quite as much more. For those were days in which anything well done by a colored man was an inspiration to all the rest of his race to whose knowledge it came.

At London, their singing in Springfield before the Synod bore fruit in the active efforts of the Presbyterian pastor in their behalf. The Sabbath was spent in Columbus, the Singers taking the place of the choir at one of the churches, and singing at a Sunday-school concert which is remembered as an occasion of special interest.

At Worthington they met a hearty welcome from Professor Ogden and his wife, their old instructors at Fisk, who had done work of lasting value in laying its foundation, but were now in charge of the Ohio State Normal School at that place. There they remained several days for much-needed rest, giving a concert meanwhile which, thanks specially to the active efforts of these two old friends, yielded $60. At Delaware their concert paid still better, and, for the first time on their trip, they were permitted to sit in the same parlors and at the same tables in the hotel as white people. Three concerts at Wellington netted them little more than enough money to take them on to Cleveland ; where they sang on Sunday at the First Presbyterian and Plymouth Congregational churches, with the satisfaction that their unique praise services invariably gave.

All this time they were living, as the old phrase has it, from hand to mouth, — depending on the proceeds of one concert to pay the next morning's hotel charges and buy their railway-tickets to the next appointment. Any special collapse in an evening's receipts left them helpless till some friend stepped forward — as there was almost always some friend in such an emergency who did — and paid hall and hotel bills.

But the great trial was that no light had dawned on their mission. They would have done better to stay at home if they were to make nothing above expenses. So scantily clad were they that Miss Sheppard was obliged to travel one rainy day with no protection for her feet but cloth slippers. It was not until some time after the biting weather of the Northern winter, to whose severity they were quite unused, had fully set in that Mr. White was able, by borrowing $5 that had been given to Minnie Tate, and picking up $19 in other ways, to purchase overcoats for two of the young men, who had really been suffering for want of them.

In one way and another a comfortable outfit had been secured for the young women ; but such were the varieties of style represented that it was not uncommon for Ella Sheppard to be asked if Minnie Tate was her daughter, — the former being twenty and the latter fourteen. And Jennie Jackson, who was nineteen, was sometimes taken to be the mother of Eliza Walker, who was fourteen.

The coolness, amounting often to indifference and sometimes to suspicion, with which even many of the warmest friends and supporters of the American Missionary Association looked upon this new agency for raising funds for its work, was one of the specially discouraging and trying features of the enterprise. Ministers were often loth, and not unnaturally, to let the Singers into their choirs ; and if they gave them the use of their churches for a praise meeting, they sometimes showed a strong inclination to take their own seats among the audience and near the door !

But Mr. White's grip upon his purpose was not easily loosened, and he learned to let none of those things move him, knowing that the enthusiasm of these doubting friends after the service was almost sure to be in about an inverse ratio to their expectations before it.

During these days of experiment and trial Mr. White was loaded down with the work of at least four men. In other enterprises of this sort — and the same plan was afterwards found to be essential to the largest success of the Jubilee Singers — it is considered necessary to have a business manager, who lays out the route, visits or corresponds with editors and public men, and arranges the general plan of the campaign. Then an advance agent goes forward and puts these plans in operation, while his alternate accompanies the troupe to take up the tickets, pay the bills, and look after the details of the evening's management. A musical director arranges the programme, drills the singers, and answers the rattling volley of questions from curious and admiring friends. And where school-girls are in the company, and especially those hitherto unused to self-care and the demands of cultivated society, a governess is needed to look after their health and deportment.

In those early days the duties of general manager, advance agent, musical director, ticket-seller, and porter all fell to Mr. White. When the Singers halted somewhere for rest, he pushed ahead to lay out a new route ; sometimes, when but a few appointments remained, he left Miss Wells and Miss Sheppard, the pianist, to attend to them while he went off to make new ones. The Singers he kept in drill the best he could. A rehearsal of some piece on their evening's programme was often the first course when they gathered about the dinner-table.

With all this work on his hands, there lay on his heart the burden of increasing debt and the consciousness that, while the business affairs of the University were needing his presence, the fact that he was earning no money and sending them no encouragement was adding to the uneasiness and anxiety of his associates at home. Many a time their last dollar was paid out for provisions; and he and they found frequent occasions to adopt the prayer of the old slave-song, —

> "O Lord, O my Lord, O my good Lord !
> Keep me from sinking down."

But with a steadfast Christian faith, that seemed little less than obstinacy to those who could not read the Divine leadings, he held on.

CHAPTER IV.

LIGHT IN THE EAST.

MR. WHITE had laid out the plan of his trip with special reference to reaching Oberlin in time to sing before the National Council of the Congregational churches, which was to assemble there on the 15th of November. Consisting, as it would, of leading Congregational ministers and laymen from all parts of the land, and specially representing the constituency of the American Missionary Association, he argued that to get a hearing before it would give him leverage of great advantage for his work. And his reasoning was not at fault.

The Council consented to hear a few pieces during a recess in their deliberations. Everybody was delighted. A collection of over $130 was taken upon the spot ; and the seed sown was destined to bear much richer fruit after many days. Two of the secretaries of the Association were present, and they agreed that it was advisable for Mr. White to push on eastward. To relieve him of some of his overload of care, Mr. G. S. Pope, formerly in the service of the Association in its work among the freedmen, but now a theological student at Oberlin, was engaged to attend to the duties of advance agent.

From Oberlin the company went to Cleveland to

give two concerts in Case Hall. The churches had
been filled the Sunday before to listen to the Singers, but at neither concert were the receipts sufficient to meet expenses. Before the close of the
second evening's entertainment, on Saturday night,
Mr. White made a few remarks explaining their
mission, declaring his faith that God had called
them to the work, and would somehow open the
way; but frankly admitting that he had barely
money enough to pay for the hall, and nothing with
which to meet their hotel bills over Sunday and
their expenses to Columbus, where they were advertised for a concert. Before leaving the hall one
gentleman sent up a check for $100, written on the
back of a programme, and three others handed him
$40 more.

This gave encouragement at a time when encouragement was never more needed. For it is to
be remembered that the movements of the Singers
involved great expense. Case Hall rents for $75 a
night; to advertise a concert in such a city costs
from $25 to $50; and the hotel bills of the company
were usually from $20 to $25 a day. There was
abundant use, it will be seen, for the $140.

At Columbus came two concerts, again, which did
not pay expenses. Rev. H. S. Bennett, the pastor
of the church at Nashville to which some of the
Singers belonged, and also a trustee of the University, was present, and a prayer meeting was held to
seek the Divine guidance in deciding what should
be done with the enterprise. No light was found
on any other course but to go forward.

Hitherto the company had had no distinctive name.

They had been mentioned in a Cincinnati paper as "a band of negro minstrels who call themselves Colored Christian Singers." It was at Columbus, after an anxious and almost sleepless night, that Mr. White decided to name them "THE JUBILEE SINGERS." The Old Testament "year of jubilee" had always been the favorite figure of speech into which the slaves put their prayers and hopes for emancipation. Their year of jubilee had come — this little band of singers was a witness to it, an outgrowth of it. There was thus a suggestiveness and obvious fitness in the name — it had a flavor of its own. There was a musical euphony in it, too, and it "took" at once.

Only those who have made a study of catering for the public taste can realize how much there is in a name. A novelist knows that the sale of a new story depends almost as much upon its title as its plot. Those who have been most closely associated with the Singers have come to believe that Mr. White's christening of his company was the best night's work he ever did.

At Zanesville, also, their concert did not meet expenses. But a friend paid their hotel bill, which amounted to $27. What figure it would have reached had not the six girls been put into a single room over a shed, where the bedclothing was so offensive that they were constrained to roll the most of it in a bundle and lay it on the porch while they slept wrapped in their waterproofs, is not known.

Mount Vernon was their next point, where Rev. T. E. Monroe, who had met them at Columbus, welcomed them heartily to his church on Sunday, and aided to make their concert on Monday evening a decided success. Here Ella Sheppard, who had been for some time in poor health, became so ill that the physician advised that she return at once to Nashville. But Mr. White could not be made to believe that the Lord wanted the company to go East without their pianist, and declined to follow this advice. And in a few days she recovered sufficiently to resume her work.

Feeling their way to the best method of raising money, the experiment was tried again, at Mansfield, of a free concert with a collection at its close. But the result was the same as almost invariably attended this expedient before and since — the house was full, the contribution boxes nearly empty. On the next night an admission fee was charged, but the audience was small. Some thoughtful friend was moved, however, to propose a collection, and it enabled Mr. White to pay all bills and buy tickets to Akron, where they had an appointment for a concert on the evening of Thanksgiving Day. This yielded only $20, but the consideration with which they were treated at the hotel, and the fine Thanksgiving dinner which was set before them, made their memories of Akron very pleasant ones. At Meadville, Pa., their Sabbath services in the Methodist Church were well attended, and their concert on Monday evening moderately successful.

Still moving eastward, they came next to Jamestown, N. Y., where the Congregational pastor, Rev. Col. Anderson, who was familiar from personal inspection with the good work that was being done at Fisk, had made ready for them. A praise meeting at his church was followed, on the next two nights, by concerts. In spite of a severe snow-storm, which interfered greatly with street travel, the net receipts were sufficient for the purchase of tickets to New York city.

Stopping at Elmira, they held a praise meeting on Sunday afternoon in the First Presbyterian Church, to the disgust of a few of its supporters who spelled negro with two g's, and stayed away from the service, and to the great delight of all who attended. In the evening they sang a few selections at the Rev. T. K. Beecher's regular service in the opera-house; and the next night gave a concert at his church, which was the greatest success, so far, of their trip. The leading hotels of the city had, it is true, one after another refused the party entertainment when they arrived on the midnight train. But the papers were lavish in praise of their services of song, and Mr. Beecher wrote a letter to his distinguished Brooklyn brother, Henry Ward Beecher, warmly commending them to his attention.

The night had been long and dark, but it really seemed as if these flashes of light in their Eastern sky meant that the sunrise was at hand. At New York they were at the headquarters of the American Missionary Association, and so in a special sense among their friends. As no good hotel accommodations could be secured at reasonable rates, three of the officers of the Association, who lived in adjoining houses in Brooklyn, took the party into their own families. And there they found a home for the next six weeks.

Prior to their arrival at New York, Rev. George

Whipple, the senior secretary of the American Missionary Association, had arranged with Rev. Henry Ward Beecher that they should attend his Friday evening prayer meeting and sing a few slave-hymns at the close of the service. Mr. Beecher and his people were delighted. After singing about twenty minutes, the party started to retire from the platform. Mr. Beecher, jumping up, requested them to return. Standing in front of them, with pocket-book in hand, he indicated, with characteristic drollery and enthusiasm, that a collection would be taken up, after which they would have a few more songs. Before the meeting closed he announced that this was but a foretaste of what was to come : the Singers were to give a concert in the church the next week, and the congregation were to give them a benefit.

As Mr. Beecher's lecture-room talks were widely circulated through the papers, this resulted in a very favorable introduction to the public. The concert at Plymouth Church was well attended, and the enthusiasm unbounded. Mr. Beecher had urged his people from the pulpit the preceding Sabbath to give the Singers a hearty welcome, and they seemed bent on gratifying him to the utmost. The New York "Herald" headed the column containing its report the next morning " Beecher's Negro Minstrels." This helped to advertise their work, while it did not prejudice it in the minds of the Christian people whose opinion was worth most to it.

The experience of the next few weeks was as uniformly encouraging as that of the last two months had been depressing. A few songs in a prayer meeting or Sunday-school, with a brief explanation

of their mission, generally secured at once the offer
of the church for a concert, and a hearty commenda-
tion of their work from the pulpit that rarely failed
to bring out an audience.

From Dr. Talmage's and Dr. Cuyler's prayer
meetings they went away richer by generous contributions on the spot. Dr. Storrs gave up his Sunday
evening service for their praise meeting. Dr. Scud-
der invited them into his church. A concert in Dr.
Burchard's church, the Thirteenth Street Presbyterian of New York, was thronged by a delighted audience of the highest culture and social position.
Dr. Budington interested himself in promoting the
success of a concert in his church in Brooklyn. At
the Tabernacle Church, Jersey City, of which Rev.
G. B. Willcox, a member of the Executive Committee
of the American Missionary Association, was pastor,
they were greeted by the largest audience that had
ever yet attended one of their paid concerts — the
receipts amounting to nearly $740.

Preliminary to a flying trip to Boston to give a
concert in the Music Hall, in connection with the
annual Methodist Reunion, Mr. Beecher wrote to a
Boston friend: "They will charm any audience,
sure; they make their mark by giving the 'spirituals'
and plantation hymns as only they can sing them
who know how to keep time to a master's whip.
Our people have been delighted." And in a lecture
which he delivered in Boston just before their com-
ing Mr. Beecher took occasion to advise everybody
to attend.

Dr. Cuyler wrote to the New York "Tribune" of
their concert in his church, the Lafayette Avenue

Presbyterian of Brooklyn : " I never saw a cultivated Brooklyn assemblage so moved and melted under the magnetism of music before. The wild melodies of these emancipated slaves touched the fount of tears, and gray-haired men wept like little children. Their wonderful skill was put to the severest test when they attempted 'Home, Sweet Home,' before auditors who had heard those same household words from the lips of Jenny Lind and Parepa. Yet these emancipated bond-women — now that they know what the word 'home' signifies — rendered that dear old song with a power and pathos never surpassed. Allow me to bespeak a universal welcome through the North for these living representatives of the only true native school of American music. We have long enough had its coarse caricatures in corked faces ; our people can now listen to the genuine soul-music of the slave cabins, before the Lord led his children 'out of the land of Egypt, out of the house of bondage ! ' "

The news of their successes at this metropolitan centre of business enterprise, social culture, and Christian work, rayed out, of course, in every direction. Thenceforward a part of the heavy load that they had previously carried steadily grew lighter, — the labor of creating a *demand* for their entertainments wherever they offered them. Their enterprise was nearly out of debt, and the company were in that excellent working order which such an inspiriting change in their prospects might be expected to promote. A campaign through the principal towns of Connecticut was planned. Rev. G. D. Pike, one of the district secretaries of the American Missionary Association, as well as its other officers, had been actively interested in the work in and about New York. As Connecticut was in his district, he offered the Singers his services on this trip, which his special acquaintance with the field, as well as his business tact and energy, made most welcome. High hopes were cherished that they might be able to raise $500 a week above their expenses.

CHAPTER V.

THIS campaign was a succession of triumphs. The Singers, with their experiences of the last three months so vividly in remembrance, seemed to themselves to be walking in a dream. Mr. White had expected success, but even he had not dared to hope for such a success as this. Ministers everywhere — and especially those who had cheered the Singers at Oberlin with their applause and contributions, and so felt a sort of proprietary interest in the work — gave themselves enthusiastically to promote arrangements for their concerts. And the audiences that crowded the churches and halls where they sang did not seem to be content merely with contributing an admission fee to their funds.

Almost a *furore* for making them presents broke out, and spread from town to town as they went. At Bristol, famous for its manufacture of clocks, a gentleman pledged a supply of that useful article for the new Hall on its completion. At Winsted, another manufacturing centre, a few friends promised a bell. The Douglass Manufacturing Co., at Middletown, asked the party to take from its catalogue whatever goods the University might need. The Meriden Britannia Co. gave them a full outfit

3

of silver ware for the dining-hall ; another Meriden firm contributed gas fixtures ; and a president of one of the Meriden banks sent word that while he could not invite them to take as much as they might need from the bank, yet if they would call he would make them a present of $100.

Several gentlemen in Birmingham contributed $50 each to fit up a "Birmingham Recitation Room" in the new building. At the concert in Waterbury, two gentlemen sent up $200 ; and the contributions, in cash and valuables, at the concert in New Haven amounted to $500.

Here at New Haven the enthusiasm seemed to touch high water mark. Two of the principal hotels had declined to entertain the Singers on account of their color. The fact became public through the papers, and some of the families of highest social position in the city at once opened their doors to receive them. Their concert was announced for Thursday evening. By Tuesday morning all the desirable seats were sold. Rev. Henry Ward Beecher was advertised for a lecture on the same night. But there was so little demand for the tickets that Thursday's papers announced that the lecture would be deferred on account of the concert ! Mr. Beecher attended the concert and made one of his felicitous speeches. No one was apparently more delighted than he that a day had come in that university city when a company of freed slave singers could draw an audience away from the greatest preacher and lecturer in the land.

The admission receipts at this concert were over $1,200. The collection taken for them the next

Sunday evening, in the Second Congregational Church in Norwich, was the largest contribution they had ever received at a Sunday service, and the gross income of the last seven days of this Connecticut campaign exceeded $3,900.

At the Sterling House, in Bridgeport, the party were assigned to some of the best rooms in that first-class hotel, and admitted to the same privileges in the dining-room as the most aristocratic guests. The answer of the proprietor, when asked if his boarders complained of such attentions to colored people, was pithy and to the point, "*I* keep this hotel, sir!"

At Norwich they were the guests of Connecticut's distinguished War Governor and Senator, the late Hon. William A. Buckingham. But the very next day they were turned out of a hotel in Newark, New Jersey, by a publican who would have felt honored by even a bow from Governor Buckingham on the street. This tavern-keeper had inferred, it seems, when accommodations were engaged for them in advance, that they were a company of "nigger minstrels." Although they had already retired to the rooms assigned to them before he discovered that their faces were colored by their Creator, and not with burnt cork, he promptly drove them into the street.

The outrage was the harder to bear because they were in special need of rest ; for they had been riding all night, and their nervous energies were well-nigh exhausted after the draft which the unusual excitement and success of the last few weeks had made upon them. The best citizens of Newark

visited their indignation without stint on the landlord. Some of his most valuable patrons immediately left the house; and it is said that the city
council took advantage of the favorable feeling
toward colored people thus stimulated to pass an
ordinance opening to them all the privileges of the
public schools.

A visit to Washington followed, which was no
exception to the success which had of late so steadily attended them. The Vice-President, with his
family, and many members of Congress, came to
their concerts. The President turned aside from
pressing public duties to give them audience at the
White House, assure them of his interest in their
work, and hear them sing, "Go down, Moses."
"Parson Brownlow," the famous Unionist senator
from their own State, was so ill as to be unable to
sit up, but received them in his sick-room, and cried
like a child as these emancipated slaves sang that
pleading, pathetic song of sorrow, —

> "O Lord, O my Lord, O my good Lord!
> Keep me from sinking down."

Returning again to New York, a series of concerts
culminated in two memorable gatherings at Stein-
way Hall. The platform each evening was occupied
by some of the most eminent divines of the metropolis, and the great hall was filled with a delighted
audience in which the *élite* of the city was largely
represented. Many went away unable to obtain
seats.

By this time the business methods and machinery
of concert work had been thoroughly perfected. Mr.
Pike was relieved from the duties of his secretary.

ship to continue in this enterprise, for which he had shown such aptitude, and which was to owe so much of its subsequent success to his energy and sagacity. There was need that Miss Wells should return to her school in Alabama; and Miss Susan Gilbert, who had been for some years in the service of the Association in North Carolina, and afterwards at its home office, took her place.

The Singers at last had the tide in their favor. They were now so well known that they did not need to sing to half-filled halls until they could make a reputation. Their songs were unique, and people did not tire of hearing them over and over again. Thanks to Mr. White's unusual skill, both in choosing voices and drilling them, their singing, as all the critics agreed, was something wonderful in its harmony, power, and bell-like sweetness.

Their history as emancipated slaves touched the interest and sympathy of the public, particularly that part of it which had been interested in the great anti-slavery struggle. And last, but by no means least, in accounting for their success, they furnished a refined and wholesome entertainment, which Christian people who did not care to visit the theatre and kindred places of amusement could attend and enjoy. There was need of, and a wide demand for, just such healthful and elevating diversion as these concerts afforded.

Beginning with several concerts in Boston, they now visited successively the more prominent points in Massachusetts and Rhode Island, and a number of places in Maine, New Hampshire, and Vermont, meeting everywhere an enthusiasm and a helpfulness from friends not unlike that by which they were borne through Connecticut the month previous.

Among the presents received in Boston was a $1,000 organ for the University, from Smith Brothers. Hon. A. C. Barstow of Providence had heard them at Oberlin, and tendered them the use of his beautiful music-hall at that city, where their concerts were one repeated ovation. Returning to the same city some days subsequently, after singing at Worcester, Lawrence, Lowell, Lynn, Wakefield, Andover, Cambridgeport, Taunton, and other points, another concert yielded them about $1,000.

At Andover and Taunton the good-will of the people took the shape of contributions for the purchase of books for the University library. Reaching Boston again, $1,235 was taken in at a *matinée* on Saturday afternoon, the largest sum ever realized up to that time from the admission receipts alone of any one entertainment.

Their songs, which had been written out for the first time by Prof. Theodore F. Seward, the distinguished teacher and composer, and published in book form, were sold by hundreds at their concerts, and hills and valleys, parlors and halls, wherever they went, were vocal with the Jubilee melodies.

After a week spent in Cambridge, Chelsea, Salem, and Newburyport, they visited Portland, Maine, where the Council tendered them the free use of the city hall. Remunerative concerts followed at Concord and Hanover, New Hampshire ; St. Johnsbury, Vermont ; and Springfield, Massachusetts, the latter yielding $1,050. With a night at Troy, New York, and another at Poughkeepsie, the first season's singing campaign closed. The fruit of these three months' work was $20,000, more than three times as much as their enthusiasm had dared hope for when starting out from New York on the Connecticut campaign.

It was a tired but light-hearted party that now started homeward. They had bought first-class tickets from New York to Nashville, and on arriving at the station in Louisville early in the morning, entered the unoccupied sitting-room assigned to first-class passengers. A railway employee coming along soon afterwards, gave notice that "niggers" were not allowed in that room, and ordered the party out. Mr. White claimed the right to keep his company there by virtue of their tickets, and declined to leave until turned out by some responsible authority. Thereupon a policeman was brought, who, with angry profanity, ejected them from the room, amid the applause of a cursing mob of one or two thousand people. The superintendent of the road, however, as he has made a habit of doing ever since when the party have had occasion to pass on his line, placed a first-class car at their disposal. The novel sight of such a carriage with colored faces at almost every window made a sensation at every station where they stopped.

The company was received at the University with a joy and thanksgiving that cannot be described. They had gone forth weeping; but they returned bringing their sheaves with them — a marvelous harvest after those months of marvelous patience, privation, and triumph.

CHAPTER VI.

THE SECOND CAMPAIGN.

UNDER God's blessing their labors had saved the University from suspending, or even curtailing, its work. But their success, so far, in raising money, was chiefly valuable as evidence that a way had been found for obtaining the much larger sum that the necessities of the growing work required. The Singers had received an invitation to participate in the second World's Peace Jubilee, to be held in Boston in June. Stopping in Nashville little more than a week, they again took the field. Giving a few concerts in Illinois, Michigan, and Ohio, they went on to Boston. Parts had been assigned them on the programmes of several days' exercises. The immense audience of 40,000 people was gathered from all parts of the land ; and the color prejudice that had followed the Singers everywhere reappeared here in the shower of brutal hisses that greeted their first appearance. But the air of that radical New England city is not kindly to colorphobia, and a deluge of applause answered and drowned the insult. And a day or two after the Singers had a proud revenge.

Mrs. Julia Ward Howe's stirring lyric, " The Battle-hymn of the Republic," was on the programme,

to be sung to the air of "John Brown." The first
verses were to be taken by some colored singers of
Boston. But for some unexplained reason the key
was given to the orchestra in E-flat, cruelly high
under such circumstances, and the first verses were
a painful failure. The Jubilee Singers were to come
in with the verse beginning

"He hath sounded forth the trumpet that shall never call retreat."

Fired by the remembrance of their reception on
the previous day, and feeling that to some extent
the reputation of their color was at stake, they sang
as if inspired. Mr. White's masterly drill had made
easy to them the high notes on which the others had
failed. Every word of that first line rang through
the great Coliseum as if sounded out of a trumpet.
The great audience were carried away on a whirl-
wind of delight ; the trained musicians in the orchestra bent forward in forgetfulness of their parts ;
and one old German was conspicuous, holding his
violoncello above his head with one hand, and whack-
ing out upon it his applause with the bow held in
the other.

When the grand old chorus, " Glory, glory, hallelujah," followed, with a swelling volume of music
from the great orchestra, the thunder of the bands,
and the roar of the artillery, the scene was inde-
scribable. Twenty thousand people were on their
feet. Ladies waved their handkerchiefs. Men threw
their hats in the air, and the Coliseum rang with
cheers and shouts of " The Jubilees ! The Jubilees
forever ! " Mr. Gilmore brought the Singers from
their place below, and massed them upon his own
platform, where they sang the remaining verses.

Mr. White has never quite forgiven himself that he did not answer the thunderous encore that followed with "John Brown" in the original version! Musically speaking, it was the greatest triumph of their career, and they never recall it yet without a gleaming eye and quickened pulse. It was worth more than a Congressional enactment in bringing that audience to the true ground on the question of "civil rights."

The number of the Singers had been increased to fourteen, with a view to division into two companies when it was desired to visit the smaller places where it would not pay to take the full number; and the rest of the summer was spent in rest and drill at Acton, Mass. A faithful trial, during the fall, of the experiment of two small companies little more than paid expenses; and at New Year's Day the troupe was reorganized, to consist of eleven members, as follows : Ella Sheppard, Maggie L. Porter, Jennie Jackson, Mabel Lewis, Minnie Tate, Georgia Gordon, Julia Jackson, Thomas Rutling, Edmund Watkins, Benjamin M. Holmes, and Isaac P. Dickerson.

A busy and successful campaign of three months followed. The Singers received a letter, drawn up at the suggestion of their distinguished and faithful friend, Hon. George H. Stuart of Philadelphia, and signed by such representative citizens as Mr. Stuart, Jay Cooke, Rev. Dr. Hawes, Bishop Simpson, Rev. Dr. Newton, John Wanamaker, etc., inviting them to visit that city.

The Academy of Music, one of the finest halls in the United States, had been refused a few months before for an address by a United States senator, because he was a black man. But the names of the distinguished citizens by whose invitations the Singers came to the city were sufficient to secure it for their concerts; and the fact that they were the first representatives of the colored race to occupy that platform gave a special significance to the occasion. The great building was thronged night after night, and it was one of the most profitable series of concerts ever given by the Singers.

Application had been made to several of the leading hotels for the entertainment of the party. But no hotel-keeper had been found with the convictions and courage to risk the odium he might incur if he admitted colored guests, and they had been compelled to take up inconvenient and insufficient quarters in a small boarding-house. This fact being mentioned at one of the concerts, the proprietor of the Continental, the best hotel in the city, who was absent when application was made at his office, at once announced that the Singers were welcome to as good accommodations as his house afforded. Subsequently he entertained them in the best manner, and at a generous reduction from regular rates.

While stopping at the Continental, the housekeeper one day kindly escorted the party on a semi-subterranean tour through the kitchen and other working departments of the great hotel. They were much interested in the novel sight, and asked permission to invite the working force of the hotel to their dining-room, that they might sing for them. Word came to the guests of the hotel of what was going on, and they gathered about the doors of the crowded room, begging that the concert might be adjourned to the larger dining-room. The Singers acquiesced on condition that their invited hearers, white and black, should have the front places. There probably was never a Jubilee concert that gave more pleasure to the occupants of the "reserved seats;" nor to the rest of the audience, for that matter.

At a concert to be given soon after, in the Masonic Hall, Baltimore, a city noted for its intense pro-slavery feeling, the ticket-seller, acting in accordance with Baltimore usages, had taken upon himself the responsibility of refusing to sell reserved seats to colored people. This came to the ears of the company when they reached the city the day of the concert, and one of the Singers was sent *incognito* to the ticket-office to buy a reserved seat, and test the truth of the story. His application for a seat to hear himself sing was refused!

Here was evidently a call to do a little missionary work, as well as furnish some entertainment for the people of Baltimore. The ticket-seller was relieved from further duty, and notice was immediately given that any well-behaved person could have any seat in the hall by paying the advertised price for it. A few colored people occupied reserved seats here and there on the main floor, but it was never heard that any one received harm from such a radical innovation in Baltimore customs. The audience were apparently so interested in the singing that they forgot to study the color of their neighbors' faces.

The Singers were accustomed to being refused entertainment at hotels because of their color. This was not always, however, for fear merely of offending other guests. In one case, in Illinois, the hotel servants squarely refused to wait on the "nagurs," as *they* pronounced the word, and the Singers were their own boot-blacks and chamber-maids. At another hotel the landlord met a similar refusal by paying the mutineers their wages and sending them *en masse* into the street.

But the most offensive manifestation of caste prejudice that ever flaunted itself in the face of the party occurred during this campaign, at Princeton, N. J. They had been invited by President McCosh, and other members of the Faculty of Princeton College, to visit the place, and one of the churches had been tendered them for their concert. A little while before it was time for the concert to begin, they learned that an out-of-the-way corner of the church had been set aside for colored people, and that they were refused admission to any other part of the house. An estimable lady, who was a teacher in a colored mission school, had bought reserved seats for her class ; but they, too, were compelled to take their place in the colored quarter under the gallery, regardless of the contract involved in the tickets which they held. The Singers were so indignant that they would gladly have given up the concert. The fact that so many old friends of the slave had come from long distances to hear them alone persuaded them to go on.

During two seasons of concerts they had never before been subjected to this indignity, even in a public hall ; that it should be offered in a church of Christ was a grievance not to be passed over in silence, and Mr. White took occasion, in an interval of the concert, to characterize it in the terms it deserved. It was plainer preaching on *that* subject, probably, than had ever been heard in that church before. And most of those who greeted it with their angry hisses have doubtless already lived long enough to be heartily ashamed of them.

A tract of twenty-five acres, on a commanding site overlooking the city of Nashville, had been purchased for the permanent location of Fisk University. During the war the eminence had been crowned by Fort Gillem, one of the encircling line of fortifications that had defended the city in the memorable contests that had raged around it. The students had worked with the laborers to level the earthworks, and the foundations had been laid for a noble building for university purposes, to be called Jubilee Hall.

The project of visiting England with a view to raising funds for its completion, had been for some time under prayerful consideration. During the winter campaign it was decided to start early in the spring, and the closing work of the season took the shape of farewell concerts in New York, Brooklyn, Boston, Providence, and elsewhere. One given in Boston, March 26th, in response to a request signed by Governor Claflin, Wendell Phillips, William Lloyd Garrison, Rev. E. E. Hale, Dr. Kirk, Phillips Brooks, and several other eminent citizens, was the most successful, financially, that the Singers had ever given in that city.

And so the winter's work drew to a close. Its net result was the addition of another $20,000 to their fund, making $40,000 that they had now secured.

With exultation and thankfulness as they thought
of past success, and with high hopes for the future,
preparations were at once made for the visit to Great
Britain. Very cordial letters of introduction, commending the music and mission of the Singers, were
given by the governors of five of the New England
States, Rev. Henry Ward Beecher, Hon. George H.
Stuart, George MacDonald, — then on a lecturing
tour in America, — and other influential friends. An
open letter from Governor Brown of Tennessee, be-
speaking favor for their work, was especially valuable
as coming from the chief magistrate of a common-
wealth that was so recently a slave State.

They were not to get away, however, without still
another conflict with caste prejudices. Cabin ac
commodations were refused the party by one after
another of the leading ocean steamship lines. At
last an application to the Cunard agents at Boston
met with ready success; and when the Singers
stepped on the deck of the good steamer Batavia, it
was to enter upon a year's experience where such
annoyances were to be unknown.

CHAPTER VII.

THE FIRST VISIT TO LONDON.

A STUDY of the situation, on Mr. Pike's arrival in London in advance of the Singers, made it at once apparent that the indorsement and patronage of distinguished people, which had been such a helpful feature of the work in America, were still more indispensable to an early and large success in England. Under a favoring Providence, the letters of introduction previously mentioned speedily opened the way to all of the assistance of this sort that could have been hoped for.

The Earl of Shaftesbury, than whom no man in any station, on either side of the Atlantic, has given his life more untiringly and unselfishly to every species of philanthropic effort, at once manifested much interest in the enterprise. There was no one else in the kingdom whose rank, relations, and reputation would combine to make him such a valuable patron and friend. He was President of the Freedmen's Missions Aid Society, the English organization auxiliary to the American Missionary Association. In accordance with his advice, arrangements were made for a private concert at Willis's Rooms on the afternoon of the 6th of May. Cards of invitation, issued in the name of the Earl of Shaftesbury and the Committee of the Society, were sent to the nobility, members of Parliament, the leading clergymen of different denominations, editors, and other persons of influence likely to be interested in such a cause. The visit to London had been timed with a view to reaching the influential ministers and laymen from all parts of the kingdom who throng there during the May anniversaries. Mr. Pike — and Rev. James Powell, who, being of English birth and used to English ways, had come with him to aid in launching the enterprise in foreign waters — had spent nearly a month in stirring up an interest through the press and in private effort.

When the time for the concert came the hall was filled with a distinguished assemblage. The Singers, keenly eager to justify the promises made on their behalf, did their best.

Before the programme was half finished they had carried their audience by storm. At the close congratulations were lavished upon them, and offers of coöperation were abundant. The Duke and Duchess of Argyll were foremost in expressing a desire to assist them, and, before leaving the hall, arranged for a visit of the Singers to Argyll Lodge the next day. The leading dailies, the "Times," the "Standard," the "News," the "Telegraph," on the next morning gave cordial praise of the entertainment. Through this first concert, and the distinguished hospitalities to which it led, the Singers found themselves at once introduced to the British public under the most favoring auspices.

The visit to Argyll Lodge was destined to be a more notable event than they, even in their great

4

gratification at what was apparent in the invitation,
could at all foresee. The kind attentions with which
they were received in the drawing-room were strikingly in contrast with their experiences of recent
date in American hotels and railway stations. But
what was their surprise and delight to learn, after a
little time pleasantly spent in conversation with
their noble hosts and other guests, that the Queen
had been asked to be present and was expected
soon !

They had been told, again and again, that if they
could but sing before the Queen their success would
be assured. But how to secure her notice for a
company of young freed people, singers who had
nothing of more renown to offer than the prayer-
meeting hymns which they had learned in bondage,
was a problem on which no light whatever had been
cast until it lay suddenly solved before them.

Soon after her Majesty's arrival the Duke informed them that she would be pleased to see them
in an adjoining room. At his request they sang,
first, " Steal away to Jesus ; " then chanted the
Lord's Prayer, and sang " Go down, Moses." The
Queen listened with manifest pleasure, and, as they
withdrew, communicated through the Duke her
thanks for the gratification they had given her.
There was no stage parade or theatric pomp in the
scene ; but the spectacle of England's Queen coming
from her palace to listen to the songs which these
humble students learned in their slave cabins, and
that not merely for her own entertainment, but to
encourage them in their efforts to lift up their fellow
freed people, was worthy a place in history.

Other hospitalities made the next three months of their stay in London memorable. Probably no private party of Americans was ever before treated with such distinguished attention. It was not possible for them to accept all of the invitations of this nature which they received. While at Argyll Lodge Dean Stanley invited them to visit the Deanery at Westminster Abbey, a pleasure which they realized a few days after.

An afternoon was spent at the delightful home of Samuel Gurney, the distinguished Quaker abolitionist, near Regent's Park, introducing the Singers to a large party who were Friends in truth as well as name. To no one did the mission of the Singers mean more than to the noble circle of Quakers, who had all their lives long been such devoted friends of the oppressed.

Mr. George MacDonald, the distinguished novelist, gave them a welcome invitation to his beautiful home on the banks of the Thames, on the occasion of one of his annual garden parties — a scriptural gathering of the poor and the lame whom he brings out from the crowded London tenements every summer for a day's outing under the trees. No one could have enjoyed more than the Singers the opportunity of contributing to its success.

But the most distinguished attentions of this sort which they received came through the kind offices of Rev. Newman Hall, in mentioning the Singers to Mr. and Mrs. Gladstone. The latter were to give a lunch at their residence, Carlton House Terrace, to the Prince and Princess of Wales, and other members of the royal family. The Singers were invited to be present and chant the Lord's Prayer, as a grace before lunch, and contribute in any other way that might seem desirable to the entertainment of the occasion. Standing in one of the alcoves of the dining-room, they had been unobserved by most of the company until the sweet harmony of that fine Gregorian chant stole through the room. Then explanations passed from one to another of the guests, and there was a call for more singing. Along with other pieces, " John Brown " was given, awakening that special enthusiasm with which English hearers have always received it. The Prince of Wales, looking over the book of songs, called for " No more auction-block for me;" and Mrs. Gladstone asked, as a special favor to the Grand Duchess Czarevna, whose imperial father-in-law had emancipated the serfs in Russia, that " John Brown" might be repeated. Special interest was manifested in the Singers, and many questions were asked of them, and many encouraging words spoken by the distinguished guests. Among those present, beside the royal family, were the Duke of Sutherland, the Duke and Duchess of Argyll, Earl Granville. and other members of the nobility ; Count Munster, Mr. Motley, and other representatives of the diplomatic corps ; the Hon. John Bright, the Bishop of Winchester — son of the great Wilberforce, Mrs. Jenny Lind Goldschmidt, and others.

But this was not all of their good fortune at the hands of the Prime Minister. A few days after a note was received, in which Mr. Gladstone said, " I beg you to accept the assurances of the great pleasure which the Jubilee Singers gave on Monday to

our illustrious guests, and to all who heard them. I
should wish to offer a little present in books in ac-
knowledgment of their kindness, and in connection
with the purposes, as they have announced, of their
visit to England. It has occurred to me that perhaps they might like to breakfast with us, my family
and a very few friends, but I would not ask this
unless it is thoroughly agreeable to them." The
note closed with suggesting a day on which he would
be glad to entertain the party.

The invitation was of course gladly accepted.
Aside from the especial help it might give them in
their immediate work, it was felt that such attentions to a company of colored people, just out of
bondage, by the Prime Minister of Great Britain,
was a rebuke to the caste spirit in America that
would do great good. Their first visit to Carlton
House Terrace was to entertain its guests, now they
were to be themselves its guests. Mr. Gladstone
had spent the night at Chiselhurst, and was in such
poor health that he had, by his physician's order,
excused himself from attending the banquet to be
given at the Mansion House that evening by the
Lord Mayor to the Ministry. Nevertheless, he rode
in twenty-five miles that morning to keep his appointment to meet his negro friends at breakfast.
Several members of the Cabinet and of Parliament,
with ladies of the nobility, were also among the
guests. The Singers were distributed between them
at the table, and were the recipients of the kind and
assiduous attentions of all. Writing an account of
the occasion for the New York "Independent," the
Rev. Newman Hall, alluding to the color prejudices

of so many Americans, said: "I wish they had been present yesterday, to see Mrs. Gladstone and her daughters, and the noble lords and ladies present, taking their negro friends by the hand, placing them chairs, sitting at their side, pouring out their tea, etc., and conversing with them in a manner utterly free from any approach either to pride or condescension; but exactly as if they had been white people in their own rank in life. And this not as an effort, nor for the show of it, but from a habit of social intercourse which would have rendered any other conduct perfectly impossible."

After breakfast Mr. Gladstone showed to his guests some of the principal objects of interest in his collection of art treasures, explaining them in his fascinating style. "Then," to quote Mr. Hall's account once more, "all the party being gathered in the drawing-room, the Jubilee Singers entertained us with their wonderful music. First we had 'John Brown.' I never heard them sing it as they did yesterday. It was not the music alone, but the features of the singers also which made it so impressive. Their eyes flashed; their countenances told of reverence and joy and gratitude to God. Never shall I forget Mr. Gladstone's rapt, enthusiastic attention. His form was bent forward, his eyes were riveted; all the intellect and soul of his great nature seemed expressed in his countenance; and when they had finished he kept saying, 'Isn't it wonderful? I never heard anything like it!' The tender, thrilling words and music of 'Oh, how I love Jesus!' brought tears to the eyes of the listeners; and when they closed with the Lord's Prayer, all the company, led by Mr. Gladstone, reverently stood with bowed heads in worship.

" Just before leaving the room, they sang, 'Good-by, brother ; good-by, sister ; ' which went to every heart. As brothers and sisters, the Premier and Mrs. Gladstone, with their guests, bade them farewell. It was just noon when we passed through the hall, where several persons were waiting on official business, to see the Premier, who, doubtless, from that time till late at night was anxiously occupied with public affairs, but whose morning was given up to his negro friends with such heartiness and leisure of mind that a stranger might suppose he was, of all present, the one whose time was most his own."

Subsequently Mr. Gladstone sent them a valuable present of books for the University library ; as did Mr. Motley, in accordance with a promise made to them on their first visit to Carlton House Terrace.

Several other occasions served to introduce the Singers to the public, in a way that gave them special assistance in their work afterwards. By the kind assistance of Dr. Allon, and one or two other friends, arrangements were made for them to appear at the annual dinner of the Congregational Union. Six or seven hundred leading ministers and laymen, from all parts of the kingdom, were present, and gave rapturous applause to one after another of the songs. As at Oberlin, this served as a favorable introduction to the denomination throughout the whole country. The promises of coöperation were many and were well kept.

At the anniversary of the Freedmen's Missions

Aid Society the Singers were advertised as one of the attractions, and the hall was much too small to hold all who came. Lord Shaftesbury presided. The venerable Dr. Moffat was among the speakers, and eloquently testified to the renewed hope he had for Africa as he listened to the Jubilee Singers. He had been "holding his tiny rushlight amidst the desolations of that continent, and holding it with the feeling that his efforts were almost futile." But as he thought of the trained missionaries who might yet be raised up among the emancipated slaves of America, he saw light ahead. Here again the "John Brown" song electrified the audience. As the stirring refrain rang out,

"John Brown died that the slave might be free!"

the dense audience rose to their feet, hats and handkerchiefs waved in the air, and the deafening applause was kept up until the Singers answered with "God Save the Queen."

The American Missionary Association, in its work among the freedmen, had always taken strong ground against the use of liquor — a position which Christian people in England do not always take. The National Temperance League therefore looked upon the Singers as allies in its work, and gave them a cordial welcome to their annual *soirée* at the Cannon Street Terminus Hotel. Such was the eagerness to hear them, after they had filled the parts assigned them on the programme, that the other exercises were shortened to give them more time for singing.

At the great annual fête of the League at the Crystal Palace in July, the free use of the opera-house was tendered to the Singers for a concert, and all the advertising was done for them by the committee, without charge. The great event of this occasion, which was attended by thousands of excursionists from all parts of the kingdom, was the concert given in the central transept, by a choir of five thousand children, under the management of Mr. Frederick Smith. The audience was immense. At the close of the programme the Jubilees came upon the platform and sang one or two songs. One of them, of course, was " John Brown," and at the last verse Mr. Smith suddenly rapped up his army of singers to join in the chorus. The effect was very fine, and the song closed with round after round of long-continued applause.

These occasions, however, added little to the Jubilee Fund, valuable as they were in the way of advertising for their future work. The best method of raising money was, in fact, a perplexing question. Friends generally advised free concerts with collections at the close. But experience with this plan in America was not at all encouraging. And, with one or two exceptions, in the few cases where it was tried the collection did not usually yield them more than one half as much as would have been received if the same audience had paid the common price for tickets. One of these exceptions was a concert of a semi-private character, planned by Dr. Allon, and given in his chapel at Islington. Special cards of invitation were sent out, on which the mission of the Singers was explained, and the fact stated that a contribution would be taken up for their work. Of this concert Dr. Allon wrote to Rev. Henry Ward

Beecher : " The desire to hear them was so great that three times the number of tickets ·printed were applied for. There was a great and most enthusiastic crowd. The collection produced about £80. Since then the interest in them has been growing, and they will certainly have a hearty reception now that they are about to visit the provincial cities and towns of the kingdom. Their songs produce a strange, weird effect. Notwithstanding the occasional dash of negro familiarity and quaintness of expression, they are full of religious earnestness and pathos, and one loses all sense of oddity in the feeling of real and natural piety. It will greatly help them that their performance is such as the most fastidious will not hesitate to welcome in our churches." Dr. Allon's high standing, both as a Christian minister and as an editor of works to promote the service of song in the churches, gave to his testimony special value.

The singing in the Nonconformist churches being generally congregational, there seemed to be no opportunity for the Singers to take that special part in the Sabbath services to which they had become so much accustomed in America, and in which it was believed that they had done no little good. An invitation from Rev. Newman Hall, therefore, to sing at his morning service in Surrey Chapel was specially welcome as opening the way to such work. They were seated near the pulpit, and their singing both before and after the sermon seemed to be regarded by the congregation as every way befitting the Lord's house and its worship.

There were special reasons why it would be better

to give concerts in public halls, where the people of all denominations could meet on a common footing and with equal interest in the work. But it was foreseen that it would often be impossible to secure suitable assembly-rooms of this sort. And as it was by no means common to open even Nonconformist chapels to gatherings where an admission fee was charged, Mr. Hall was again of timely service to the company by his offer of Surrey Chapel to them for a paid concert. A crowded audience attended, and the precedent thus established was of much value.

Concerts were given in these days at St. James's Hall and other places of repute for first-class entertainments. But the expenses were so large as to eat up most of the receipts. The concerts in chapels paid better, enlisting as they did, in the case of strong city churches, a corps of co-workers in the congregation who were usually sure to fill the house.

The most notable of these was the one given in Mr. Spurgeon's Tabernacle. Mr. Spurgeon had signified, in his hearty way, his interest in their mission, and had tendered them the use of his large church. The Sunday previous to the concert they attended service there, and at the close tarried to shake hands with the great preacher. While waiting their turn in the room adjoining that where Mr. Spurgeon receives his visitors, some of the people present asked for a song. The Singers, with tender and earnest feeling, sang, "O brothers, don't stay away." They had scarcely finished when Mr. Spurgeon summoned them into his room. He had heard the song, and was so affected by it that he wanted them to attend the evening service and repeat it there.

"I do not know whether you will approve or not," he said to his people in commencing the service, "but it seems to me it is the right thing, and I will take the risk. After the morning service I heard the Jubilee Singers sing a piece, 'O brothers, don't stay away, for my Lord says there's room enough in the heavens for you.' I found tears coming in my eyes; and looking at my deacons I found theirs very moist too. That song suggested my text and my sermon to-night. Now, as a part of the sermon, I am going to ask them to sing it, for they preach in the singing; and may the Spirit of God send home this word to some to-night — some who may remember their singing if they forget my preaching."

Then followed the singing, so clear and strong as to reach every person in the great audience of five or six thousand people, and Mr. Spurgeon preached with great effect from the text, "It is done as thou hast commanded, and yet there is room." In giving notice of the concert on Wednesday, he added the exhortation, "O brothers, don't stay away." And his counsel was well heeded. It was advertised that the doors would be open at seven o'clock, but long before that the crowds about the gates were such that it was necessary to open them to avoid blockading the street, and the attendance was estimated at seven thousand. Every song, with the inspiration and enthusiasm of such an audience, was a triumph.

At the close Mr. Spurgeon said : " Now our friends are going to Scotland, and I have told them to come

here and hold their first concert when they return to
London. They have come to Great Britain to raise
£6,000 : they will do it ; and if they want £6,000
more, let them come back to this country again, and
we will give it to them."

CHAPTER VIII.

THE Singers had spent over three months in London, and arrangements were now made for a tour in Scotland, with a visit to a few of the larger cities on the way.

Hull, the birthplace of Wilberforce, was reached, by a pleasant coincidence, on the first of August, the anniversary of emancipation in the British colonies. Here it was decided to try the plan adopted at Dr. Allon's chapel in Islington, and find how it would work in the provinces. Fifteen hundred invitations to a concert in the Hope Street Chapel were sent out to those most likely to be interested. The collection, which seemed a very large one to the friends who had charge of the arrangements, amounted to about £52. When it was explained that not less than £100 ought to be realized from each evening's work, if the mission to Great Britain was to be a success, some of the good friends insisted on another trial, with an admission fee. When the time came, Hengler's Cirque, in spite of a rainy evening, and to the delight of all, was crowded, and the receipts were £140.

Sitting by his window at the hotel in Hull on Sunday evening, and noting the tide of people flow-ing idly by, Mr. White proposed an extempore religious service for their benefit. Taking the base of the King William monument as a platform, Mr. Pike preached and the Singers sang of the love of Christ to a crowd that filled the street farther than the voice of either speaker or singer could be heard. Tears trickled down the cheeks of many to whom the sound of prayer or religious song was apparently almost unknown.

In Scarborough, a free concert yielded a collection of about £90, and on Sunday the Singers sang, in a heavy rain, to a Sunday-school gathering of four thousand people on the green. At Newcastle, Rev. H. T. Robjohns had so thoroughly worked up the public interest that every seat was sold before it was time for the concert to commence. At Sunderland, Moody and Sankey had been holding meetings not long before, at the beginning of what afterwards became such a famous work, and the special interest thus awakened in religious song prepared the way for the Singers. J. Candlish, Esq., M. P., presided, the ministers of the different denominations were advertised as patrons, and the large Victoria Hall was filled before many who wished to attend could obtain admission.

Lord Shaftesbury, with characteristic kindness and foresight, had given the Singers a cordial letter of introduction to his friend, John Burns, Esq., of the Cunard Steamship Line, at Glasgow. Mr. Burns's sympathies were at once awakened, and he arranged for a garden party at Castle Wemyss, his residence on Wemyss Bay. Invitations were sent out to four hundred persons of prominence and influence in the west of Scotland ; and Lord Shaftesbury, who was also present, made a very effective appeal for their coöperation in promoting the mission of the Singers.

To crown these helpful efforts to forward their work in Scotland, his lordship placed in Mr. Pike's hands, before their departure from Castle Wemyss, letters of introduction to the Lord Provost of Glasgow, and the Lord Provost of Edinburgh. Their contents were at that time unknown. Least of all was it suspected that they contained a proposal that the authorities of Glasgow and Edinburgh should vote a welcome to the Singers, and bring them before the public under the auspices of the " Lord Provost, the magistrates, and the Town Council " of these two leading cities ! Reports of this gathering at Castle Wemyss had prominent place in the daily papers, kindling a general desire to hear the Singers.

A series of successful concerts followed. At Largs the pastor of the Established (Presbyterian) Church set a desirable precedent by opening his church for a concert with an admission fee. The city authorities at Greenock gave the Singers the use of the town hall, which holds two thousand people. It was densely crowded on two evenings with audiences as sympathetic and enthusiastic as could be desired.

As this was the season when many of the people of the larger towns in Scotland were at the summer resorts, it was decided to pay a short visit to Ireland. Letters from Mr. Burns, and the indorsement of the Hon. George H. Stuart, who is held in high regard in that country of his birth, prepared the people to welcome them. Dr. Henry, President of Queen's College, presided at the first concert in Ulster Hall, Belfast, and Rev. William Johnson, the Moderator of the General Assembly, aided heartily in the subsequent work there. At Londonderry their welcome accorded with the historic fame of that old, liberty-loving town, so foremost in Protestant zeal and good works.

Returning to Scotland, they were met with the announcement that the authorities of Glasgow had acted upon Lord Shaftesbury's suggestion, and voted to invite them to give a concert at the city hall under their official patronage. Looking backward to the bondage and ostracism that was still so fresh in their memory, such a thing, in that great city of five hundred thousand people, seemed almost incredible. The city hall was full. The Lord Provost presided, and beside him, on the platform, sat the magistrates and leading clergymen of the city. The Singers were eager to do their best, and the Lord Provost in his closing remarks declared that he " never attended a more delightful meeting."

Their reception at Edinburgh was equally hearty and inspiring. The authorities gave them a vote of welcome. The Lord Provost presided at their first concert, and afterwards gave a dinner-party in their honor at his own residence. At Paisley a most helpful friend was found in Sir Peter Coats, whose name as a thread manufacturer is a household word throughout the world, but whose highest praise where he is personally known is his Christian philanthropy. He entertained the Singers at his country-house on the banks of the " bonny Doon," piloted them in visits to the many places of historic and poetic interest in that vicinity, attended personally to the preliminary arrangements for and presided at their concert. At Kilmarnock, Ayr, Aberdeen, Perth, Dundee, and other cities, concerts were given that were a series of triumphs. Many presents were made in money and books for the University, and the people everywhere vied with each other in showing a most gracious hospitality.

From the first the Jubilee music was more or less of a puzzle to the critics ; and even among those who sympathized with their mission, there was no little difference of opinion as to the artistic merit of their entertainments. Some could not understand the reason for enjoying so thoroughly, as almost every one did, these simple, unpretending songs. This criticism led to the publication, by Mr. Colin Brown, Ewing Lecturer on Music in the Andersonian University, Glasgow, of a series of articles, analyzing this style of music, in which he said : " The highest triumph of art is to be natural. The singing of these strangers is so natural that it does not at once strike us how much of true art is in it, and how careful and discriminating has been the training bestowed upon them by their accomplished instructor and leader, who, though retiring from public notice, deserves great praise. Like the Swedish melodies of Jenny Lind, it gives a new musical idea. It has been well remarked that in some respects it disarms criticism, in others it may be truly said that it almost defies it. It was beautifully described by a simple Highland girl, — 'It filled my whole heart!' The richness and purity of tone, both in melody and harmony, the contrast of light and shade, the varieties of gentleness and grandeur in expression, and the exquisite refinement of the *piano*, as contrasted with the power of the *forte*, fill us with delight, and at the same time make us feel how strange it is that these unpretending singers should come over here to teach us what is the true refinement of music, make us feel its moral and religious power."

The labors of the Singers in connection with the meetings of Messrs. Moody and Sankey were one of the most memorable features of this visit to the North. They first met the evangelists at Newcastle-on-Tyne, and for some days lent daily assistance in the great work. Their songs were found to be especially adapted to promote the revival. One incident in connection with one of the noonday prayer meetings, of which Mr. Moody often spoke afterwards, cannot be better told than in the words of Rev. Mr. Robjohns : "The Jubilee Singers had been specially prayed for. A moment's pause, and there went up in sweet, low notes a chorus as of angels. None could tell where the Singers were, — on the floor, in the gallery, or in the air. The crowd was close, and the Singers — wherever they were — were sitting. Every one was thrilled, for this was the song they sang, —

> ' There are angels hovering round
> To carry the tidings home.'

The notes are before us as we write, simple enough, — the words, too ; but one should hear the Jubilees sing them. It was like a snatch of angelic song heard from the upper air as a band of celestials passed swiftly on an errand of mercy." And he adds : "Nor are these all our obligations to our beloved friends. They have gone in and out the churches, Sunday-schools, and mission-rooms, singing for Jesus. Such services to souls and Christ have opened wide the people's hearts, and the Jubilees have just walked straight in, to be there enshrined for evermore."

In the great work at Edinburgh, also, the Singers rendered special assistance, sometimes taking part in as many as six meetings a day, — prayer meetings, inquiry meetings, Bible readings, preaching services, etc. On one Sunday evening Mr. Moody preached, and they sang, to an audience of between six and seven thousand working-people, gathered by special cards of invitation in the Corn Exchange, which was followed by an inquiry meeting, at which some seven hundred asked for prayer.

After the engagements of the Singers took them away from Mr. Moody, missionary and revival meetings were frequently held on Sundays ; and at them and at Sunday-school gatherings Mr. Dickerson and Mr. Rutling — as well as Mr. White and Mr. Pike — often made addresses.

January brought a very whirl of work and a harvest of money, in connection with the campaign through the midland counties. Wherever the Singers went they met crowded houses at their concerts. Many subscriptions were made to furnish rooms, at a cost of £10 each, in Jubilee Hall. Mr. Frederick Priestman, though carrying the cares of an extensive business of his own, interested himself in perfecting arrangements for a private concert at Bradford,

which was so well worked up that it yielded £150,
Sir Titus Salt, who was unable to be present, sending
£25. Under the patronage of Rev. Eustace Conder
and Edward Baines, Esq., M. P., the first concert at
Leeds, in a pecuniary point of view, was the most
successful one so far that had been given in the
kingdom. At Halifax, John Crossley, Esq., M. P.,
the great carpet manufacturer, pledged a supply of
carpets for Jubilee Hall. One of the results of a
second visit to Hull was the presentation, for the
library of the University, of a fine oil portrait of
Wilberforce, purchased through a subscription by
the citizens, a memento of the Jubilee work that will
always be held in high regard. The Hon. John Bright
was absent from home when the Singers visited
Rochdale, but his family subscribed £10 to furnish
a room to bear his name ; and afterwards he wrote a
letter commending their mission as "one deserving
of all support," which went the rounds of the papers
and was of much help to them. At Bolton, J. P.
Barlow, Esq., gave £50 for five rooms, one of them
to be named after President Charles G. Finney, of
Oberlin College, in remembrance of his evangelistic
labors during a great revival in that town years
before.

At Manchester they were fortunate in enlisting
the services of Mr. Richard Johnson, the apostle of
ragged schools. No town was ever before more
thoroughly plowed with advertising and sown with
information, and such work never yielded a better
harvest. The proceeds of the four concerts in the
Free-Trade Large Hall amounted to over £1,200.
This sum was further swollen by the sale of the books

giving the history of their first American campaign,
the profit on these sales in one evening being £40.
Three concerts followed in the Philharmonic Hall
at Liverpool, with large receipts, the first one yielding £325. The total receipts of the month of January amounted to £3,800, or about $19,000!

But this success was achieved at the cost of an
appalling amount of work. Requests for concerts
flowed in from all parts of the kingdom. It was
impossible to comply with half of them, and the
investigation involved in deciding where to go was
an exhausting strain on time and strength. A vast
amount of correspondence was unavoidable in reply-
ing to invitations to breakfasts, dinners, and teas,
and in answering the many requests that came for
concerts for the benefit of schools, churches, asylums,
and charities of every sort. Much thought had to
be given to the preparation of newspaper notices and
other advertising, and much time had to be spent in
enlisting the interest and assistance of those whose
patronage would be valuable. Adding to all this the
incessant demands in meeting the thousand details
of concert management and hotel arrangements, and
the watchful guidance of the Singers in this new life
to which they were so unused, it is no wonder that
one after another of the working force broke down
under the load.

Miss Gilbert, whose labors had been as incessant
as they were invaluable, was taken very ill, and
obliged to give up all work. Mr. Pike, who had
been doing the work of two men, succumbed next to
serious nervous prostration, and had scarcely settled
down for the rest that was imperatively necessary,

when his only assistant gave way under the load that he was carrying, and was forbidden by his medical adviser to give any further attention whatever to business.

Mr. White was thus left alone. His lungs were weak, and the heavy fogs and the night-work were telling seriously upon them. And at this juncture came word that his wife, whose health had not been good, and who, with her children, was in lodgings in Glasgow, was ill. Yet as the gross income of the concerts at that time was averaging $1,000 a night, and it seemed to be so manifestly "now or never" with their mission, he felt that it was his duty to keep on, at whatever sacrifice of personal feelings or strength, with the work. But a few days after he received intelligence that impressed him with the conviction that his wife, who had been taken with typhoid fever, was more seriously ill than he supposed. Hurrying to her bedside, he reached it less than two days before she died. She had been a valued teacher with him at Fisk before their marriage; and her death, which would have been a terrible blow at any time, in these peculiar circumstances of his health and work was unspeakably trying. A loss of sleep and appetite followed which so reduced his strength that he was finally obliged to give up work. And in the midst of this prostration he was attacked with hemorrhage of the lungs, and for some time seemed to be lying at the very gates of death.

These facts becoming known to friends interested in the work, offers of assistance were numerous, and by relying largely on volunteer help, the Singers were able to go on and fill all their appointments.

At Sheffield, Derby, Wolverhampton, Norwich, Ipswich, Cambridge, Leicester, Nottingham, Birmingham, and other cities, the experiences of January were repeated in crowded audiences, generous contributions, and the good cheer of true English hospitality.

There was a large harvest still ungathered when the time drew near that had been fixed for their return to America. But circumstances were such, especially the health of those who had the charge of the work, that a longer stay than was originally proposed was impracticable.

A trip to the south of Wales, with concerts at Newport, Cardiff, Merthyr Tydvil, and Swansea, was followed by successful visits to Bristol, Southampton, Bath, Brighton, and a few other cities. Mr. Spurgeon, not forgetful of his farewell words when they left London, not only opened his Tabernacle to them for a second concert, but made one of his happiest addresses in connection with the present of a full set of his works for the library. The house was densely crowded, and the receipts exceeded even those of the first concert in the same place.

The closing concert was given in Exeter Hall, and yielded a larger sum than any other of the whole campaign in Great Britain. That steadfast friend, the Earl of Shaftesbury, presided. Dr. Allon, whose counsels had been of great value to them from the beginning, gave the audience some account of the winter's work. Nearly £10,000 had been raised for the Jubilee Hall, aside from special gifts for the purchase of philosophical apparatus, and donations in money for the library, and of books from Mr.

Gladstone, Mr. Motley, Dean Stanley, Mr. Spurgeon, Mr Thomas Nelson, and many other friends.

Lord Shaftesbury, in his parting address, spoke with much feeling of the pleasure their visit had given the English people, and of the affection and respect in which they would always hold the Jubilee Singers. The Doxology was sung by the entire assembly, and his Lordship, amid the cheers of the audience, and in their behalf, bade them good-by, shaking hands with each of the Singers as they left the platform.

To the Singers personally, aside from the financial success that had attended their work, the visit had been one of almost unalloyed satisfaction. They had been everywhere the object of hospitable attentions that, if they had any fault, were sometimes so urgent and abounding as to be wearisome, after the strain which their work made upon their energies. Few of them had suffered from sickness, and the shorter distances to be traveled, and the warmer temperature in winter, had made concert-work easier than in America. In no way were they ever offensively reminded, through look or word — unless by some rude American who was lugging his caste conceit through a European tour, or by a vagrant Englishman who had lived long enough in America to "catch" its color prejudices — that they were black.

The Singers reached Nashville in time to attend the Commencement exercises. The trustees passed resolutions testifying to the interest and sympathy with which they had followed their career, to their industry and devotion in their work, and to the high honor they had achieved for themselves and their people, adding : " No one can estimate the vast amount of prejudice against the race which has perished under the spell of their marvelous music. Wherever they have gone they have proclaimed to the hearts of men in a most effective way, and with unanswerable logic, the brotherhood of the race."

CHAPTER IX.

In 1875 Fisk University completed its first decade. During the ten years thousands of young people had been gathered in its classes. Its students, in turn, had taught tens of thousands in Sabbath and day schools, communicating far and wide among the freed people its uplifting influences. It had conquered the respect of those who began by hating it. It had opened to the vision of vast numbers of colored people new possibilities of Christian attainment and manly achievement. It had demonstrated the capacity of that despised race for a high culture. It had raised up the Jubilee Singers, who had done great things for their people in breaking down, by the magic of their song, the cruel prejudice against color that was everywhere in America the greatest of all hindrances to their advancement; who had raised the money to buy a new site for the University, and erect on it a substantial and beautiful hall to take the place of the tottering hospital barracks; and who stood on the threshold of its second decade as its special and providential reliance in laying the foundation of its needed endowments.

This year was marked by several events of special interest. Hitherto the University had been without a president. Its work had been outlined and guided in its general features by the American Missionary Association. It was felt that the time had come when a capable president should take charge of it, supported by a fully-organized faculty. For this place, Rev. E. M. Cravath was the unanimous first choice of its trustees and friends. More than any one else he had had the responsibility of its establishment ; and, during his subsequent service for several years as field secretary of the Association, the burden of planning its work and providing for its wants had rested chiefly upon him. Educated at anti-slavery Oberlin, and identified all his life with anti-slavery effort, he was felt to be specially adapted and providentially guided to the place. And as soon as events shaped so that he could well be spared from those duties, he resigned his secretaryship in the Association and entered upon the new work.

In 1875, also, the University graduated its first college class. It had taken some of them, ten years before, with little more than a knowledge of the alphabet, and carried them through extended preparatory studies and a thorough classical course, to the point where a rigid examination awarded them the degree of A. B. At graduation one was chosen instructor in the University, and others found responsible positions awaiting them as teachers in the city schools at Nashville and Memphis. Two were the sons of an unlettered freed woman, who had consecrated every spare dollar of her hard earnings, for these ten years, to aid her boys in getting an education. It was a proud hour for her when they stepped upon the stage to receive their diplomas —

a scene that it would have done the heart of every contributor to Fisk University good to see.

The completion and occupancy of Jubilee Hall was another of the important events of 1875. Both in its architectural appearance and substantial construction of the most durable materials, as well as in its admirable adaptation to the permanent uses of the University, it is all that could be desired. Its walls are of brick, with stone foundations and facings; every part of the work upon it has been done in the most thorough manner, and it is believed to be the best building of its kind in the Southern States. Crowning a commanding eminence overlooking the capital city of Tennessee and the beautiful encircling valley of the Cumberland, it stands, not only an enduring and most fitting monument to the toils and triumphs of the Jubilee Singers, and to the sympathy and generosity shown them by the Christian public on both sides of the Atlantic, but a perpetual inspiration to the freed people as they struggle out of the slough of ignorance and social proscription in which emancipation found them.

But the very success of these years had increased the demands upon the University faster than it had supplied the means of meeting them. It had achieved results that demonstrated the necessity of its existence and guarantied its permanence. But its needs were greater than ever. Its new site, and the new hall standing upon it, was simply the solid foundation for future growth, and it was entirely without the means, within itself, of supporting, to say nothing of enlarging, its work. Money was urgently needed for endowments from which to provide for the support of teachers and to aid earnest, struggling students to educate themselves for Christian work as teachers and ministers of the gospel. In the poverty of the freed people the revenue from tuition fees could be but a trifle at the best, compared with its expenses.

The continual financial pressure throughout the country caused a serious shrinkage in the receipts of the American Missionary Association. Many who were wont to give liberally to such objects were unable to do so longer. Urged by these pressing necessities, and convinced that God pointed out the way by his providences, the Jubilee Singers, after a few months of rest, again took the field. Mr. White's health was still so seriously impaired that it was impossible for him to undertake such exhausting work as was involved in the entire care of a concert campaign, and Prof. T. F. Seward, of New York, who first wrote down the Jubilee Songs, and had been deeply interested in the work, was fortunately secured to share the labor.

A series of concerts was given during the winter and spring in the larger cities of the North, preliminary to another tour abroad. Some of them were very successful, but the net receipts of the winter's work were not large. The "times" were hard; the weather was unusually cold and unfavorable; and rival companies, some of whom appropriated not only the name, but even the testimonials belonging to the Jubilee Singers, had taken the field, and, to a considerable extent, had trampled down the harvest where they had not the ability to gather it.

On May 15th the company, reorganized to consist

of ten members, sailed for England in the Cunard steamer Algeria. It was a sign of progress that more than one steamship line, which had refused them cabin accommodation two years before, offered reduced rates if they would accept them now. Mr. White accompanied them, to give, so far as his health would permit, the counsel and assistance which his previous experience made so valuable, and President Cravath followed in the autumn to take charge of the general interests of the enterprise, and to reinforce the working force when the heavy drafts of the busy season began.

The announcement that they would be present and sing a few of their slave-songs at the annual meeting of the Freedmen's Missions Aid Society, in the City Temple, London, Monday evening, May 31st, was to many of their friends the first news of their return from America ; but it was news that traveled quickly, and it drew an audience that not only packed every inch of space in that capacious church, but filled the large lecture hall below with an overflow meeting.

So great was the gathering about the building that to get even to the doors was a formidable task, and the chairman, Lord Shaftesbury, was delayed some minutes in reaching the platform by the difficulty of penetrating the dense crowd that filled the corridors. In ascending the stand his eye caught sight of the Singers in the gallery, whom he greeted with a cordial salutation, and in his remarks on taking the chair he said : " I am delighted to see so large a congregation of the citizens of London come to offer a renewal of their hospitality to these noble brethren and sisters of ours, who are here to-night to charm us with their sweet songs. They have returned here, not for anything in their own behalf, but to advance the interests of the colored race in America, and then to do what in them lies to send missionaries of their own color to the nations spread over Africa. When I find these young people, gifted to an extent that does not often fall to the lot of man, coming here in such a spirit, I don't want them to become white, but I have a strong disposition myself to become black. If I thought color was anything — if it brought with it their truth, piety, and talent, I would willingly exchange my complexion to-morrow. In the name of this vast mass of British citizens, and, I may say, in behalf of thousands and tens of thousands who are absent, we receive them with joy again to our shores, and will do all that in us lies to advance their holy cause ; and, besides our prayers and hospitality, we will do as Joseph did to his brethren, send them back loaded with all the good things of Egypt." Rev. Dr. Parker, pastor of the City Temple, reëchoed these words of welcome in an eloquent address, and the occasion could not have been more of an ovation to the Singers than if it had been planned for that purpose.

The next evening they gave their opening concert to a large and very enthusiastic audience in Exeter Hall, with an address full of a genuine English welcome from the chairman, Rev. Ll. D. Bevan.

At this time Messrs. Moody and Sankey were in the midst of their great work in London. The Singers had not been in the city an hour before a request came from Mr. Moody that they would take part in the service that afternoon at the Haymarket Opera-house. The next day he desired them to sit on the platform, and sing "Steal Away" after the sermon. That remarkable series of meetings at the West End was drawing to a close. The house was packed in every part with an audience representing much of the wealth and rank of London ; upon whom Mr. Moody urged the claims of Christ in a discourse of peculiar tenderness and power. At its close the great congregation bowed, with tearful faces, in silent prayer. Soon the soft, sweet strains of "Steal Away" rose from the platform, swelling finally into a volume of conquering song that seemed to carry the great audience heavenward as on angels' wings. The effect could not have been happier had the song been written for the sermon, or the sermon for the song.

Thereafter their services were in almost constant demand in the London meetings. For several weeks they declined nearly all applications for concerts, in order that they might be free for this work. After Messrs. Moody and Sankey had closed their services at Bow-Road Hall to go to Camberwell, the meetings were continued at the former place, with preaching each night by the Rev. Mr. Aitken or Mr. Henry Varley, and singing by the Jubilee choir. The attendance was so large, on week-day as well as on Sunday evenings, that hundreds were sometimes turned away, even after a congregation of ten or twelve thousand had crowded into the hall.

After these meetings closed, Mr. Aitken gave them a letter testifying to his misgivings at first in employing in such a work an agency that might seem

so sensational, but cordially declaring that his misgivings were quite at fault, and that he should carry
away most pleasing recollections of their work together. In recognition of their services in these
meetings, a subscription of over £500 was made
for Fisk University by a few members of the committee having the meetings in charge. Mr. Moody
gave them an open letter to his friends everywhere,
warmly commending their mission; and before leaving the country purchased and presented to each
of the party a duplicate of that copy of Bagster's
Bible, whose almost constant use in his meetings he
has made so famous and popular.

Nothing could have better prepared the way for
their special work, nothing could have better prepared them for it, than these revival labors. The
religious papers carried reports of the meetings
throughout the kingdom ; and wherever they went
thereafter, the great Christian heart of England gave
them a specially fraternal greeting.

During July and August, months usually unfavorable to concert receipts, the appointments at various
places in Wales and the South of England drew,
generally, good audiences. It was, however, after
the fall work began in Scotland that it was most
manifest how wide-spread and hearty was the interest with which their return was awaited. Applications for concerts poured in from every quarter of
the kingdom. Full houses met them everywhere.
At Inverness, where they appeared under the patronage of the provost, magistrates, and other leading citizens, the Music Hall was much too small to
accommodate the eager crowds that thronged the
doors on two successive evenings.

At Aberdeen, Lord Kintore was active in efforts to make their visit a great success. At Dundee, Provost Cox presided at their concert, and the receipts were larger than on their first visit to that city in the high tide of enthusiasm two years before. At the first concert in Glasgow, given in the Kibble Crystal Palace, the receipts for tickets, and the profits on the sale of books for the one evening, amounted to nearly £325. At Edinburgh, where the chair was taken on one evening by Lord Provost Falshaw, hundreds were turned away from the doors of the Music Hall, even after all standing room had been exhausted.

The religious effect of their concert-work was never more gratifying nor manifest. Several of their new songs, particularly, seemed to have a peculiar power in reaching the hearts of their audiences. After one of the concerts in Glasgow, an unknown friend placed £15 in the hands of one of the Singers, as a contribution to their fund, accompanied with the request that they would sing "I 've been Redeemed " at every concert they should give in Great Britain. Their singing of this and other hymns at the Glasgow Evangelistic Conference, in October, was spoken of in all reports as one of the special attractions of that inspiring meeting. Their services were sought also at the similar Conference in Dublin a few weeks later. This was their first visit to Dublin ; and at these meetings, and at the concerts which followed, Irish enthusiasm was thoroughly enkindled. Mr. Russell, known through the three kingdoms for his efficient services to the temperance cause, gave most valuable assistance in "working up" the concerts; and at the first concert in the Exhibition Palace it was estimated that fifteen hundred applicants for tickets were turned away after every seat in the great hall was filled.

Religious meetings with the Sunday-school children, on Saturday or Sunday, came to be, also, a common and important feature of their work. Admission was always given by free tickets, previously distributed to a certain proportion of teachers and scholars; and the exercises consisted of singing, alternated with short addresses. At Aberdeen, 4,000 teachers and scholars filled the Music Hall, at nine on Sunday morning; and over 5,000 gathered in the Drill Hall, Edinburgh, at ten o'clock, on a Sunday. At Liverpool the tabernacle erected for Mr. Moody's meetings — one of the largest ever built for his services — was crowded by over 12,000 children, representing over ninety different schools. Each of these meetings, like others in smaller cities, were occasions of sweet and solemn interest that will be long remembered.

Nor was this visit any less marked than the first one for the social attentions shown to the Singers. The Earl of Kintore, Lord Lieutenant of Aberdeenshire, entertained them at his ancestral seat, Keith Hall, — whose walls were laid before the Pilgrims landed on Plymouth Rock, — and made them his debtors by the memory of the delightful day spent there and by subsequent kindly attentions. Their visit to Chester brought a pleasant note from Mr. Gladstone, recalling their former acquaintance, and inviting them to spend an afternoon at Hawarden Castle, his country home in North Wales, and pro-

posing to send his carriages to meet them at the
railway station two miles away. A memorable afternoon was spent in social intercourse with the great
statesman and his family, in the inspection of his
art and literary treasures, and in wandering about
the ruins of the older castle, — which dates back to
the days of Edward the First. No one could have
had a more gracious welcome to the hospitalities of
this historic English mansion. The Duke and Duchess of Argyll also invited them, for the second time,
to Argyll Lodge, where they met a company of distinguished guests, including the Princess Louise,
on terms of pleasantest intercourse and most friendly
interest.

It was in the midst of this year's work, and when
Jubilee Hall had been but a little time occupied, that
the need of another building at Fisk University became so apparent and imperative as to demand
immediate action. The ordinary earnings of the
Singers were all needed in meeting the other pressing necessities of the school, and much prayerful
deliberation was had concerning ways and means
for supplying this want. It was finally decided to
undertake to raise by subscription £10,000 for the
erection of a companion building to Jubilee Hall,
which should be called — with obvious fitness and
significance — "Livingstone Missionary Hall." It
was when this decision was but just reached, and
before any general announcement had been made
of the plan, that a check was received from the
Baroness Burdett-Coutts for two per cent. of the
entire sum, — £200. And Mrs. Agnes Livingstone Bruce, Dr. Livingstone's daughter, — the

loved " Nannie " of whom he so fondly and proudly
speaks in his journal, — testified to her interest in
the Singers, and to her appreciation of this trib·
ute to her father, by a handsome subscription.
Soon after this the movement was publicly inaugu·
rated in London by means of two invitation concerts, under the patronage of Lord Shaftesbury
and other distinguished friends. The chairman at
the first of these concerts, Samuel Morley, Esq.
M. P., himself subscribed £100; and under the
impetus thus given to the effort over $15,000 was
secured that year for Livingstone Hall, while concert work yielded good returns for the general uses
of the University.

Would concerts on the Continent pay? Would
the slave songs keep their power where the words
lost their meaning? These were questions that
had been asked often during the work in England.
While the Singers were taking a brief summer rest
in Geneva, Switzerland, an experiment had been
tried which, if one swallow only made a summer,
might have seemed conclusive as an answer to these
questions. Just before their departure they gave a
concert in the *Salle de la Reformation* at which Père
Hyacinthe presided. The distinguished chairman,
and, with few exceptions, the audience, did not understand English — much less the vernacular of the
slave songs. But the hall was crowded and the enthusiasm rose to white heat. When asked how they
could enjoy the songs when they could not understand the words, the answer was, " We cannot understand them, but we can *feel* them." With all the
encouragement which this concert gave, the certainty

of heavy loss if a tour on the Continent proved a failure, made the venture still seem a hazardous and doubtful one.

One of the London concerts was the means of turning the scale in which this question lay balancing. Mr. G. P. Ittman, Jr., an eminent Christian gentleman of Rotterdam, and a leading merchant there, was in London on business when his attention was attracted one day by an advertisement in the "Times" of a Jubilee concert that evening at Surrey Chapel. He attended, and was so greatly interested that he came forward at the close of the concert and urged the Singers to visit Holland, offering to do all in his power to make their trip a success. When the time came, some months afterward, to go, Mr. Ittman was found to be as good as his word. He not only gave his own time and influence lavishly in preparing the way for the Singers, but he enlisted the active coöperation of influential and generous friends all through the kingdom. The "Story" found an admirable translation at the hands of Rev. Adama van Scheltema, who rendered the songs, even, into Dutch with remarkable success. The publisher, Mr. A. van Oosterzee of Amsterdam, was one of the most serviceable helpers whom the mission of the Singers ever enlisted.

Local committees of leading citizens were formed in almost every place the Singers planned to visit, who assumed the burden of preparing for the concerts, and whose patronage was itself a guaranty of success. Where there were no halls of suitable dimensions the churches were tendered to the Singers, and even the great cathedrals, as at Utrecht, Leenwarden, Harlegen, Zwolle, Dordrecht, Delft, Alkmaar, and Schiedam were opened for their concerts. Nowhere have the Singers found a heartier welcome or left dearer friends than in the Netherlands.

The most distinguished attentions which they had hitherto received from the great and the learned were quite eclipsed in the splendor of the reception given them in the palatial mansion of the Baron and Baroness van Wassenaer de Catwijck at The Hague, where they met the Queen of the Netherlands — famous as well for her own accomplishments as the patronage she has given art and literature — and other members of the royal family, and a hundred or more of the nobility and diplomatic corps of the Dutch capital. All but the Singers were in court dress, and the files of soldiery that lined the path to the door, the liveried servants that ushered the guests to cloak-room and *salon*, the brilliant costumes of the ladies, and the no less brilliant uniforms and decorations of soldiers and diplomats, the coronet of the queen flashing with diamonds, and the rich furnishings of the elegant apartments made a scene of dazzling splendor which was only heightened by the attentions shown to their dusky guests. The Queen gave the Singers a pleasant greeting individually, and testified to the sincerity of her expressions of pleasure in listening to their songs by honoring their public concert, a few evenings later, with her presence. The King also received them, not long after, at his royal residence, the Loo, and added a generous subscription to the fund for Livingstone Hall.

After two months spent thus with their Dutch friends, the Singers returned to their work in England, their treasury the fuller by $10,000 for this excursion to the Netherlands, and their plans now taking shape for a visit to Germany.

CHAPTER X.

EIGHT MONTHS IN GERMANY.

THE field in Great Britain had been well har-
vested. The diminished receipts of concert work,
owing to the hard times which rested like a leaden
pall on English industries, warned the Singers that
the longer they delayed their contemplated visit to
Germany, the less revenue it would probably yield
them, because of the increasing stringency there.
In October, 1877, therefore, they set their faces,
not over-confidently, toward the country which is
the fatherland of Christian song, and where they
might expect that their work would meet severer
critical tests than it had yet encountered. Stopping
in Holland to sing at a few places that they were
obliged to pass by on their previous visit, they met
everywhere with attentions that made this hurried
passage through the Netherlands seem like a holi-
day excursion. Crowned heads could scarcely have
been treated with more distinction at some of the
hotels, even, where they were guests.

President Cravath had preceded them to Berlin, —
accredited by letters from their unwearied friend,
Lord Shaftesbury, to the British ambassador and
other influential personages, — to make known their
mission and prepare for their coming. To do this

with success was a delicate and difficult task. But
the speedy entrance which they found, on their arrival, into the best circles of the German capital
showed how wisely and well it had been done. Baron
von Bunsen, son of the great scholar, gave a dinner-
party in their honor, at which they met, among other
distinguished people, leading representatives of the
diplomatic corps at the imperial court. And reception followed reception in the drawing-rooms of the
élite, which made them and their mission known to
the leaders in the philanthropic, musical, and religious circles of the city, and, to some extent, of the
whole empire. One of the court preachers, Rev.
Dr. Bauer, and his estimable wife extended to them
the hospitalities of an ideal German Christian home.
The Singers were permitted to share in the Christmas festivities of the household — which were advanced several days on the calendar to give them
acquaintance with this domestic anniversary as German families delight to observe it.

But no other occasion in Berlin — nor any in their
varied experience elsewhere — was so significant or
memorable as their reception by the Crown Prince
and Crown Princess at the " New Palace " in Pots-
dam. They were invited to attend there at four
o'clock on a Sunday afternoon. German usage, in
high places as well as low, is so far removed from
the stricter views of Christian people in the United
States regarding Sunday observance, that the Singers had some misgivings about accepting the invitation. But the advice of their most judicious Christian friends was in favor of going, and the result
proved that their fears were indeed at fault. The

imperial carriages, under charge of an officer of the household, were sent for them. Arrived at the palace, there was none of the distinctive pageantry of royalty to be seen, beyond the grim troopers who stood sentinel at the doors and clanked their sabres through the corridors. After their wraps had been laid aside the Singers were ushered into an elegant *salon* — selected for this occasion, as the Crown Princess afterward informed them, because of its admirable acoustic properties. The Crown Prince and Crown Princess quickly came in to greet them, and were followed by their children and other members of the imperial family, including Prince Frederick Charles, the hero of Metz.

It was as much of a gratification as a surprise to the Singers to find that the emperor himself, who had come out from Berlin to dine at the New Palace, had detained his special train, and suspended his engagements at the capital, that he might remain longer and hear their songs. As the straight, stately old soldier entered the room he bowed pleasantly to the Singers, and, taking his place near President Cravath, asked such questions about the freed people and the mission of the Singers as gave a pleasant insight into his largeness and kindliness of heart. An aide brought him an easy-chair, to which he was well entitled by his years as well as his relation to the company, but he declined it, and, with the politeness of the old-school gentleman, remained standing during the half hour of conversation and singing that preceded his departure. Those who thus met him will never be able to think of him other than as gracious in manner and noble in character as he is eminent in imperial position.

The Singers, at intervals, sang "Steal Away," "I've been Redeemed," "Who are these in Bright Array," and others of their most effective spiritual songs. "Nobody knows the Trouble I see" filled the eyes of the Crown Princess with tears, and she apologized for seeming "so weak," saying that the thought of the wretchedness of the slave life which gave birth to such a wail as that quite overcame her. In the familiar conversation during the intervals of the singing, the Crown Princess told the Singers that she had been anxious for a long while to hear them. Her mother — Queen Victoria — had excited her interest in them by a long letter which she wrote giving an enthusiastic account, at the time, of their singing when she heard them at the Duke of Argyll's. Beyond her Majesty's courteous and formal thanks on that occasion, they had had no hint of the impression which their singing made upon her, and this intelligence, so many years after, was specially gratifying.

The Crown Prince chatted socially of matters in America, and begged a copy of the songs, saying that he should wish to play and sing them with his family. "These songs, as you sing them," said he, "go to the heart, they go through and through one." Both he and the Crown Princess not only expressed great delight in the singing, but asked of their plans for work in Germany, gave some suggestions, and expressed a hearty hope that their visit might be a very successful one. Tea was served for the Singers before their departure, and the Crown Princess brought her children forward to shake hands with each of them. It was a delightful glimpse of the home-life to-day in the palace of Frederick the Great, with its fine culture, warm feeling, and religious sincerity. In its bearing on the future work of the Singers it was worth everything. As Rev. Dr. Joseph P. Thompson said, in an account of it written for the "New York Independent," "the kindly, hearty approbation of such an audience was a certificate of character as well as of musical merit. They were received at the palace not as a strolling band of singers, but as ladies and gentlemen, and the degree of culture and politeness they exhibited were gracefully recognized by their illustrious hosts."

Subsequently the Domkirche in Berlin — the church where the imperial family worship — was tendered to them without charge for their concerts, and the Sing-Akademie — a music hall into which nothing but entertainments of high tone and the best character are admitted — was opened to them, and the concerts were every way a complete success. At their concerts in the Sing-Akademie, on their return to the capital some weeks afterwards, the Empress Augusta was present on two occasions, and sending for Professor White, during the intermission, to come to the imperial box, manifested by her many questions her curiosity to know about the history of the Singers, and her interest, especially, in the religious aspects of the work at Fisk University.

German critics, it was found, yielded as readily to the mysterious charm of the Jubilee songs as had those of other countries, and were quite as unanimous and hearty in their praise. Rev. Dr. Kögel, another of the four court preachers, and perhaps the most eloquent divine in the empire, wrote an excellent article for "Daheim," in which he spoke in the highest terms of their work. He said: "Berlin is, indeed, not Germany, as some modest inhabitants of this metropolis think, still a good part of it, and, to tell the truth, one highly critical. Should they only stand first (so said to themselves the traveling Singers from the emancipated negro-folk of North America) the fire proof of musical Germany, especially on the hard ground of the central province, then would they win the game in the more out-of-the-way parts of our German fatherland. And they have won!" And elsewhere the same writer says, "These are not concerts which the negroes give; they are meetings for edification, which they sustain with irresistible power." The "Berliner Musik-Zeitung," a severely critical journal, in a long and discriminating article took up the concert programme, piece by piece. Of "Steal Away, and the Lord's Prayer," it exclaims, "What wealth of shading! What accuracy of declamation! Every musician felt then that the performances of these Singers are the result of high artistic talent, finely trained taste, and extraordinary diligence. Such a *pianissimo*, such a *crescendo*, and a *decrescendo* as those at the close of "Steal Away" might raise envy in the soul of any choir-master." The same critique closes, "Thus the balance turns decidedly in favor of the Jubilee Singers, and we confess ourselves their debtors. Not only have we had a rare musical treat but our musical ideas have also received enlargement, and we feel that something may be learned of these negro singers if only we will consent to break through the fetters of custom and long use." And the critics of the "Volks-Zeitung," the "Bürger-Zeitung," the "Tagblatt," and the "Königliche privilegirte Berlinische Zeitung" were all of one accord in the same favorable verdict upon both the songs and the singing, as judged from artistic standards.

Now and then there would be, of course, here as everywhere, a growling discord in the general harmony of the greeting. One crusty journalist published an article disparaging their work, and declaring that their pretense of raising money for a school was probably a Yankee swindle. This served a good purpose in calling out a fine tribute to their mission from a German gentleman who was a stranger to the Singers, but who had traveled in the United States. In speaking of what they had accomplished he likened the famous "Sing-Akademie" of Berlin to a cow-shed, in architectural comparison with Jubilee Hall.

In England that earnest, evangelistic element in the churches, which stood by Mr. Moody's work, everywhere took a special interest in the Singers and prized their services of song as an effective ally in gospel effort. The same class of Christian people in Germany met them with the same fraternal heartiness, and rejoiced in this unique instrumentality for bringing gospel truth to the formalists and the materialists whom it was so difficult to reach.

After this good start at the capital the company went successively to most of the larger cities in the empire. At Wittenberg they made joyful pilgrimage to the places associated with Luther's memory, and sang "Praise God from whom all blessings flow" in his room in the old monastery. At Weimar, noted for its musical and art atmosphere, they had a crowded house, the Grand Duke and his retinue attending, with much courtly clatter of military escort. At Wiesbaden they sang in the Curhaus, the now dismantled old gambling hall, and in Homburg also the Jubilee songs echoed to the same strange associations. Visits to Göttingen, Cassel, Hanover, Hamburg, Lübeck, and other of the old free cities thereabouts, followed.

At Brunswick they sang in the hall where Franz Abt was wont to conduct concerts, and received from the great composer a cordial greeting and many attentions. Thence their appointments took them, among other places, to Osnabruck, Munster, Dortmund, Essen, Elberfeld, and Dusseldorf. At the latter city they were the recipients, after the concert, of a formal reception and fraternal address from the evangelical Protestant element of the city. At Barmen, the capital of the iron and coal district, with its large operative population, they had an overflowing house. Spending a Sunday there, they visited the great Sunday-school, one of the largest in the world, singing for the children, and listening to their singing; the name of Jesus, the name that made them one, being the only word that either could recognize in the other's songs.

At the Catholic city of Cologne, where the Protestant minority has little vigor for Christian work, their concerts were not successful. At the Catholic city of Bonn, on the contrary, where the Protestant element has more of apostolic ardor, they found full houses. Their stay at this university town is remembered with special interest for a delightful Sun-

7

day afternoon hour spent in the charming atmosphere of the great Professor Christlieb's home. In the conversation the professor spoke with enthusiasm of his pleasant experiences in the United States, during his visit to attend the meeting of the Evangelical Alliance. Just then, he said, he was reading with the deepest interest President Finney's memoirs, and making notes therefrom for use in his classes. Asking about Oberlin, he begged Professor White to say to its Faculty that its religious influence was felt and gratefully owned in Bonn University. He spoke with admiration of Mr. Finney and Mr. Moody as men of power, because they were men of positive convictions.

Their visits to Darmstadt were lifted to a high place in memory by the pleasant acquaintance they made with that most charming lady and noble woman who was so greatly beloved by every one in her royal circle, and so idolized by her people, the late Princess Alice, Grand Duchess of Hessen. The court theatre was placed at the disposal of the Singers, and the Grand Duchess attended the concert with her children, whom she spoke of in answer to a visitor's admiring glance, with motherly pride and daughterly loyalty, as the "Queen's grandchildren." The Grand Duke was absent from home at this time, and the Princess Alice expressed the hope that the Singers would be able to visit Darmstadt again, when her husband could have the opportunity of hearing them. Returning for another concert a few weeks later they were gratified to find not only the Grand Duke and Grand Duchess present in the royal box, but also the Prince of Wales and Duke of

Connaught, who had stopped at Darmstadt for a visit to their sister, on their way to London from the ceremonies of the grand royal double wedding at Berlin. After the concert the Singers were summoned to the royal box; the Princess Alice received each with a pleasant greeting, and expressed the hope that they might have continued success. The Prince of Wales spoke of the enjoyment their singing gave him at Mr. Gladstone's, asked which of the party were present on that occasion, and added the hope that they would make another tour of England before returning home.

At Dresden there was a successful concert, attended by the King and Queen of Saxony, who manifested much interest in the slave songs that were such a novelty to German ears. In Leipzig, distinguished for music and learning, their reception was all that could be desired. The Gewandhaus, in which, as in the Berlin Sing-Akademie, only the best class of concerts is allowed, was placed at their disposal, and the concerts were a great success.

A visit was made to Stettin at the invitation of a German gentleman, who was formerly engaged in business in Memphis, who entertained them in the finest manner in his elegant home. Concerts were given in Breslau, Munich, and other cities. A brief visit was made to Switzerland, and then, retracing a part of their winding track northward, they filled out their eight months' campaign in Germany.

Financially, it had not been the success that was desired. The hard times had been growing harder every month; it was expensive work to break up such new ground; and it was found necessary, in the abundance of low-priced musical entertainments in that country, to place the admission fees lower than in England or the United States. But testimony came from many sources, and in many ways, that their visit had been rich in results. It was a good thing to go up and down Germany singing Christian truth to multitudes who would have turned from it had it come in any other guise. Their visit was a revelation of the qualities and capacities of the negro to those who had known so little of him, that was in his favor. Listening to the Singers, thoughtful people said with surprise, "We could not take even our German peasantry and reach such results in art, and conduct, and character, in generations of culture, as appear in these freed slaves." Their presence and work gave, as it could be seen, an added impulse — far more than it could have done in this country — to the freshened interest that all the western nations feel in everything that relates to the exploration, civilization, and Christianization of the continent of Africa. And doubtless it was of less consequence in the Divine thought that the Singers should take away much money with them, than that they should leave such influences at work behind them.

At the close of this campaign future prospects for successful concert work abroad seemed so uncertain that it was deemed best to disband the company. Some of the Singers remained on the Continent for study, and the others turned their faces westward, for that visit home which their three years' absence had prepared them to enjoy so much.

CHAPTER XI.

PERSONAL HISTORIES OF THE SINGERS.

THE *children* who were set free by the abolition of slavery in the United States occupy a position in which no other generation, of any color, or in any land, were ever placed before. Behind them are all the disabilities and cruelties of that bondage in which their lives began. Before them are all the possibilities of culture, distinction, and usefulness that are open to the citizens of one of the foremost nations of the earth. This fact adds a peculiar interest to the personal histories of the Jubilee Singers.

With the misguidances and limitations of their early life such as they were, — and it is not possible for any one to have an adequate idea of them who has not stood face to face with them, — the readiness with which the Singers met the new social demands that were made upon them in their work was as remarkable as the quiet modesty and self-possession with which they received the attentions and honors that came so suddenly to them. It was a dizzy change from a breakfast of hominy and bacon in a slave-cabin to dinners in the mansions of the wealthy, and receptions in the drawing-rooms of the nobility. But their heads were not turned by it. They may feel more at home on the concert platform than they did at first, but their manners there have remained as natural and unaffected — as free from professional "airs," as if they had never sung outside their own school-room.

To some of them it has been a daily regret that they had to surrender their school advantages as they did. But they have made that good as well as they could by keeping up special studies and courses of reading, so far as the disadvantages of their nomad life year after year would allow.

Every member of the company is a professing Christian, one or two having been converted in connection with the religious influences that have by God's blessing ever attended the work. Whenever the exigencies of hotel life or railway travel do not prevent, family worship is held each morning — a novelty to hotel servants usually, and a season of spiritual refreshment which friends who are occasionally present refer to afterward with peculiar interest.

At different times twenty-four persons in all have belonged to the company. Twenty of these have been slaves, and three of the other four were of slave parentage. There is not room in this volume for even brief histories of all the twenty-four. Such have been selected as together give the truest idea of slavery as it was felt by the generation to which the Jubilee Singers belong; of the changes and difficulties to which emancipation introduced them; of the sympathy and assistance they need and deserve. The unembellished facts in the sketches that follow form a mosaic that brings out the dreadful pattern of slavery as no story or sermon could reproduce it.

ELLA SHEPPARD was born in Nashville. Her father, while a slave, had hired his own time, and earned enough, in carrying on a livery stable, to buy his freedom, for which he paid $1,800.

His wife was owned by a family living in Mississippi, and soon after Ella's birth she was taken back to that State. The mother was worked so hard that the baby could have little attention, and nearly died of neglect. When it was fifteen months old the father heard that it was very sick and not likely to live. Going at once to Mississippi he bought his own child for $350, and took it, ill as it was, home with him to Nashville. Afterward he tried to buy his wife, but her master refused to sell her. By and by they were entirely separated from one another. By the usage of slavery she was dead to him, and he married again.

His second wife was also a slave, and he purchased her freedom, after their marriage, for $1,300. Free papers could not be executed without going to a free State. Before it was convenient to make a visit to Ohio for this purpose, he became embarrassed in his business.

Having bought his wife, she was legally his property, and as liable to be seized and sold for his debts as his horses were. He learned one night, through a friend, that some of his creditors were intending to take her for this purpose. Without waiting an hour he hurried to an out-of-the-way railway station in the woods, some miles distant, and placed her on board the midnight train bound for Cincinnati. Soon after, he followed with his child, leaving all *the rest* of his property to his creditors, and beginning life anew, without a penny of his own, in Cincinnati.

In Cincinnati, Ella attended a colored school, with frequent and sometimes prolonged absences on account of poor health. When twelve or thirteen she began to take lessons in music. But the sudden death of her father by cholera, when she was but fifteen, broke up their home. All his property, of which he had again accumulated a considerable amount, including the piano he had given to Ella, went to pay the costs of unjust law-suits, and she and her stepmother were thrown on their own resources. Often they were in great straits, and more than once Ella went to festivals where her services as a pianist were in demand, but went supperless, because there was nothing in the house to eat.

A friend, who had become acquainted with her musical abilities offered to give her a thorough course of instruction as a music teacher, with the understanding that she was to repay him from her earnings whenever she was able to. An eminent teacher of Cincinnati was engaged to give her instruction on the piano. She was the only colored pupil, and the conditions on which she was taken were, that the arrangement should be kept secret, and that she should enter the house by the back way, and receive her lessons in a secluded room upstairs, between nine and ten at night.

The failure of her patron very soon broke up these plans. Being under the necessity of earning her own living, she accepted the offer of a school in Gallatin, Tennessee. Although she had thirty-five scholars, the remuneration was so small that she was able to save but six dollars from the term's work. With this she went to Fisk University, where she was engaged in study, and in work for self-support, for about two years, when she was appointed one of the teachers of instrumental music. She aided in drilling the choir with which Mr. White gave the cantata of " Esther," and out of which the Jubilee Singers were organized. As the skillful pianist of the company, she has been with it in all its travels.

Maggie L. Porter was born in Lebanon, Tenn. Her master was wealthy, owning some two hundred slaves, and, as her mother was a favorite house-servant, she saw little of the harsher side of slavery in her childhood.

Not long before the war her master removed to Nashville, and there the President's proclamation, and the coming of the Union army, gave Maggie and her parents their freedom. When twelve years old she began to go to school. The next year she was one of the three hundred pupils that gathered in the old hospital barracks the first week the Fisk School was opened.

An older sister had been sent away to a plantation in Mississippi before the war, and it was not known what had become of her. The mother often talked of her — told how she looked, and what she did when she was with them, and speculated about her finding her way back to them in the tide of homeless freedmen that in those days ebbed and flowed through every Southern city. Day by day, as Maggie passed the railway-station on her way to school she would scan the passengers who got off the trains, to see if there was any one among them who answered her mother's description of her missing sister. But no such person ever appeared.

One day, when Maggie was alone at home, a woman came to the door inquiring for her mother, who was out at work. Maggie had been instructed to let no strangers in when she was thus left in charge of the house, and the visitor was refused admittance. When she at last declared she was her sister from Mississippi, Maggie would not believe her. And even her mother, when she met her, did not recognize her, she had changed so much in these years of absence. It was such a disappointment to the sister that she soon returned to Mississippi, and it was some time before she could get over the chill of this reception sufficiently to come and make her home with her mother. After the war her father was persuaded to try his fortunes with a company of freedmen going to Liberia. But from the day he left, no word ever came back from him.

For two years Maggie was constant in her attendance at Fisk. Then when a call came from the Board of Education for teachers for country schools, Maggie, though scarcely fifteen, offered her services. She passed the required examination, and was appointed to a school at Bellevue, seventeen miles from Nashville. She taught during the fall, and went home to spend the Christmas vacation — always a time of hilarity, and often of disorder, in that part of the country. Returning the first Monday of the New Year, she found nothing but a heap of ashes where her school-house had stood. It was probably burned — as the easiest method of getting rid of the school — by some of those who were so bitterly opposed to efforts for the elevation of the freedmen. Her next school was twelve miles south of Nashville. Here she taught in a rough log building. It had no window except a hole in one side, closed by a board shutter, and the seats were logs split in halves and set on sticks.

When Mr. White decided to prepare his student choir to give the cantata of "Esther," Maggie's fine voice marked her for the part of Queen Esther, which she rendered with a success that surprised and delighted every one. She has missed taking her part in but few of the concerts that the Jubilee Singers have given since their first appearance in Cincinnati in 1871.

The grandfather of JENNIE JACKSON was the slave and body-servant of General Andrew Jackson, President of the United States. He and his family were set free in General Jackson's will. Her father died before her recollection. Her mother had been a slave, but her mistress at her death gave her her freedom and some little property. This was before Jennie's birth, so that she was free-born.

But emancipated slaves were looked upon with little favor by the slave-holders, and had few friends. Free colored people were forbidden by law to associate with slaves, and white people would not keep their company. There were always those who were ready to wrong them; there were rarely any to take their part. So when the trustee in whose hands Mrs. Jackson placed the property that fell to Jennie's mother appropriated it to his own use, she found no redress. He even attempted to get possession of her "free papers," that he might destroy them and re-enslave her and her family. But she buried them secretly in her garden, and no promises, nor coaxings, nor threats could bring them from their hiding-place, so long as there was danger that harm might come to them.

With so little in the old home to make it seem like home to them, when Jennie was three years old her mother removed with her four young children from Kingston, Tenn., to Nashville. In their poverty and friendlessness it was necessary for the children to help in earning their own living whenever work could be found for them. While but a child herself Jennie went out to service as a nurse girl. When fourteen or fifteen she came home to help her mother, who was working as a laundress.

As yet she had had no opportunity to attend school. It was while spending the forenoons over the wash-tub, and her afternoons in a freedmen's school, that she learned her letters. By and by she entered the Fisk School. But her mother's health gave way, and the family earnings were not large enough to allow her to study at all steadily. When their money was gone, she would leave school and go to work until some more was saved up, and she could return to her studies. She paid for her tuition by service in Mr. White's family out of school hours, and took in washing during vacations.

From childhood she had a fine voice, and delighted in singing. But her mother, with judgment as rare as it was wise, and with what seems now almost like prophetic vision, steadily refused to allow her to sing in choirs, or on other occasions where there would be danger of overstraining her voice, or to let her take lessons in vocal culture from teachers who might do it harm. "Save your voice and you may have a chance to do some good with it some day," she would say. But it surely had not entered into that unlettered freedwoman's heart to conceive how *much* good it was to do to the thousands whom it has stirred with Christian song on both sides of the sea.

Jennie was one of the girls chosen by Mr. White to sing a solo at his first concert in Nashville, and she has been with the Jubilee Singers in all their work.

GEORGIA GORDON's grandmother, on her mother's side, was a white woman of Scotch-Irish ancestry, who married her own slave. Or rather they lived together in fidelity as man and wife, the statutes of the State forbidding the intermarriage of whites and blacks according to the forms of law. They had a large family of children, who, following by slave law the condition of the mother, were free-born.

Georgia's mother inherited much of the traditional Scotch-Irish capacity and sturdiness of character. Beginning by cutting and making dresses for her dolls, she became, even while a girl, a self-taught but capable seamstress and dressmaker. She grew up without school advantages ; but at church one day, the text, which was the first verse of the Gospel of St. John, specially attracted her interest, and she committed it to memory. On reaching home she took the Bible and got some one who could read to find this verse for her. Picking out the words one by one, she learned them all by sight. Then she searched the Bible for words like them. Little by little she got the clew to new words. And so, un-aided, and unknown to any one else, she learned to read.

Marrying a slave, she was able by her trade as a dressmaker, not only to earn a living for her family and send her children to school, but she also hired her husband's time of his mistress for more than his wages would amount to, that they might all live together in their own home.

Georgia was born in Nashville. She began to at-tend the Fisk School very soon after it was opened, and would have entered its Freshman class in 1872 had she not laid aside her studies that year to join the Jubilee Singers.

THOMAS RUTLING'S early home was in Wilson County, Tennessee, where he was born in 1854. His father was sold away before his birth, and his family never heard from him afterward. His mother was in the habit of running away and hiding in the woods, in the hope of escaping from slavery. But it was never very long before she would be found, brought back, flogged, and set to work again. Whip-pings, however, proved of no avail, and she was finally sold and sent farther south. Tom was then but two or three years old, and his earliest recollec-tion is of parting with his mother — how he stood on the doorsteps as she kissed him and bade him good-by, and how she cried as they dragged her away from her children. Two or three years afterward his mistress told him one day, as he was playing around the house, that they had heard from his mother. She had been whipped almost to death, probably for another attempt to obtain her freedom ; and that was the last he ever heard from her. He had an older brother and several sisters. Some of them were also sold away, and he does not know where they are or whether they are alive.

His mistress treated him well in his childhood — as good treatment went in that system that separated families as if they were but a herd of sheep. He was kept at the house during the day to bring wood and water, and make himself useful in entertaining the children, and sent to the slave-quarters only at night. Once they discussed in his presence whether they would sell his brother, and he remembers how troubled both were, although they were very young, by the prospect of separation. Afterwards he heard his owner remark that he was sorry he did not sell *him* and put him in his pocket.

When he was eight years old he was set to work in the field a part of the time, — holding a plow that was about as tall as he was. The war had begun, and the other slaves told him he must listen sharp to what was said by the white folks, and report to them. He was the table waiter, and when they had talked over the war news his mistress would say to him, "Now, Tom, you must n't repeat a word of this." Tom would look, to use his own expression, "mighty obedient ; " but, somehow, every slave on the plantation would hear the news within an hour.

One night the report of the proclamation of emancipation came. The next morning the children were sitting in the slave-quarters at breakfast, when their young master rode up and told them they were free. They danced and sang for joy, and Tom, supposing he would have everything like his young master, decided at once what sort of a horse he would ride! They remained, however, on the plantation till 1865. Then, having heard that their eldest sister was in Nashville, Tom and his brother started off to find her. While with her he learned his letters. Then he drifted about, working at one thing and another, until he became a pupil at Fisk, where he remained most of the time for several years until he went out with the Jubilee Singers, on the first organization of the company. On their return to America in 1878 he remained in Switzerland for study, and has since been more or less engaged in evangelistic work there, in connection with his studies.

FREDERICK J. LOUDIN is a native of Portage County, Ohio. Though living in a free State, he was, from his earliest recollection, under the hateful shadow of slavery. The Northern States, though they had had the vitality to throw off the slave system earlier in their history, had still fostered the cruel prejudice in which the colored people were held everywhere as the representatives of an enslaved race. In some respects, this ostracism was even more complete and unchristian in the free than in the slave States.

Loudin's father had accumulated some property, and had given generously, according to his means, for the endowment of a college a few miles from his home. But when he asked that one of his children

might be admitted to the advantages of its preparatory department, he was coolly informed that they
did not receive colored students. His farm was
taxed for the support of the public schools, but it
was an exceptional favor of those days that his children were allowed to share their privileges. In Ra-
venna, where Loudin went to school for a time, the
seats in the school-room were assigned according to
scholarship. He was studious and quick to learn,
but when he was found entitled by the rules to a
higher seat than several members of his class, their
parents took their children out of school, in a white
heat of wrath that he should not only have a seat
beside but above them !

Converted when a lad, he was admitted to mem-
bership in the Methodist church at the same place.
He was then a printer's apprentice. His wages were
$45 a year, and he gave $5 of this to the church.
Having a reputation among his acquaintances as a
good singer, he applied, two or three years after he
became a church member, for admission to the choir.
To his surprise and indignation his application was
refused, because of his color. He made up his mind
that he was not likely to get or do much more good
in that church, and he never troubled it with his
presence afterward.

When a young man he found himself in the city
of Cleveland, and obliged to obtain lodgings for the
night. Going from one hotel to another he was refused by each in turn. It was nearly midnight, and
only one remained unvisited, and that the leading
hotel of the city. Using a little strategy here, he
led them to suppose he was a slave traveling in ad-

8

vance of his master, and they gave him a room at once, thanks to the reflected refulgence of this supposed ownership by a white man ! He could not have got one at any price had they known that he was a free man and paid his own bills.

There was one college in Ohio, that at Oberlin, which admitted colored students to the same privileges as white ones, and his parents would have gladly aided him in obtaining a college education. But the obstacles in the way of using it, either as a means of usefulness or of earning a livelihood, were so great that it seemed to them not worth the while. In those days the most a colored man could look forward to was a position as waiter or hostler in a white man's hotel ; or possibly, if he was exceptionally thrifty and subservient, to the ownership of a small barber's shop. After he had learned the printer's trade, in fact, he found it of no use to him. White printers would not tolerate the presence of a black compositor, and he was obliged to seek other means of getting a livelihood.

Going to Tennessee after the war, he became interested in the work of the Jubilee Singers, and joined them previous to their second visit to Great Britain in 1875.

MABEL LEWIS was born, as she supposes, in New Orleans. But of her parentage, and the date of her birth, she knows nothing beyond vague supposition. She has reason to think that her mother was a slave and her father a slave-holder, and that it was owing to the interest her father felt in her that she was sent North, when two years old, and carefully reared in a wealthy family. Her earliest recollection is of a pleasant home, of being sent to and from school in the family carriage, and of being carefully guarded even from association with the servants. But, when she was about ten years old, for some unknown reason there came a change in the treatment which she received. The family, who had used her as kindly as if she were their own child, went abroad, and left her to the care of the servants. Their cruelty and neglect were such that she finally ran away to escape her sufferings at their hands. She drifted about from one place to another, a homeless, friendless waif, cursed by the slight strain of negro blood that appeared in her hair and complexion, working as she had opportunity, and as well as she knew how, for her board and clothes. A benevolent gentleman in Massachusetts finally became interested in her, and provided her with school advantages. Other friends afterwards aided her in obtaining the special instruction in music which her fine voice deserved, and finally introduced her to the Jubilee Singers, whom she joined in 1872.

Her health gave way during the exhausting labors of their first visit to Great Britain, and she was unable for several years to take up again the exacting duties of concert work.

MINNIE TATE'S parents were both free colored people. Her grandmother, on her mother's side, was a slave in Mississippi, but her master gave her and some of her children, including Minnie's mother, their freedom. Designing to make their home in a free State, the family took such of their possessions

as they could carry in bundles on their heads, and
started on foot for Ohio, little realizing how long a
tramp they had undertaken. They had to work for
their living as they went along, and often stopped
several months in a place before they could get
enough money saved to warrant them in again taking up ·their pilgrimage. Finally they reached a
German settlement in Tennessee, where the good
people treated them so kindly that they decided to
bring their journey to an end, and make their home
among them. Minnie's mother was allowed to attend school with the white children, and obtained
quite a good education in the common English
branches. Afterwards she removed to Nashville,
where she married, and where Minnie was born.

Her mother gave her her first lessons in reading
at home, but when older she went to Fisk School.
She was one of the original Jubilee Singers, and the
youngest of the company which made the first visit
to Great Britain, where her sweet voice and her
youth drew to her many friends. On the return to
America, she was obliged, by the prostration of her
voice, to give up singing, and resumed her studies.

BENJAMIN M. HOLMES was a native of Charleston, South Carolina. He was born of slave parents
in either 1846 or 1848, but which year he never certainly knew.

When a little fellow, scarcely old enough to look
over his employer's bench, he was apprenticed to
learn the tailor's trade. His father had learned to
read a little, and secretly taught him his letters. He
studied the business signs and the names on the

doors when he carried home bundles for his master, and asked people to tell him a word or two at a time, until by 1860 he found himself able to read the papers very well. His mother then promised him a gold dollar if he would learn to write. This was not so easy as to learn to read, as asking help in any way was more likely to excite suspicion. But when sweeping out the shop, before business hours in the morning, he would study the letters in the measuring book, and so in time learned to write. He secretly taught his fellow-slaves, and came to be looked upon as one of those slaves who "knew too much."

When Charleston was threatened with capture by the Union troops, in 1862, his master, fearing they would get their freedom, sold his slaves to a trader, who confined them in the slave-prison until he should be ready to take them into the interior. While in prison Holmes got hold of a copy of President Lincoln's proclamation of emancipation. Great was the excitement and rejoicing as he read it aloud to his fellow-captives. Finally he was sold to a merchant of Chattanooga, Tennessee, who gave him a few hours before starting in which to say good-by 'o his mother, whom he never saw afterwards.

His new owner took him into his own store, and soon came to place great confidence in him. He would often say, "I'd trust any part of my business to Ben." In 1863 he and all his clerks were drafted into the rebel army, and Ben carried on the business for a short time until his owner and one of the clerks were exempted from service.

Near the end of this year Chattanooga fell into the hands of the Union troops, and Holmes took advantage of the terms of the proclamation which he had read the year before in the Charleston slave-pen. He hired out as a servant to General Jefferson C. Davis, of the Union army, at $10 a month, but in the spring returned to the employ of his old owner, who offered him $30 a month. Afterward he worked for a year or two as a cashier in a large barber's-shop, and on the death of his employer he was made administrator of his estate — the first colored man ever appointed to such duties in the State of Tennessee. He had previously taken an interest in the business, but on settling up the estate it was found to be insolvent; and after it had eaten up $300 of his small savings he gave up the business.

He had been anxious for a long while to get a better education, and in 1868 began studying at Fisk University. The next year he was engaged to teach one of the State schools for the colored people in Davidson County, and was promised $30 a month. His school averaged an attendance of sixty-eight scholars, but those were days of poverty in private, and mismanagement in public affairs, and Davidson County failed to pay him $150 of his wages. The attempt to educate the colored people met with bitter opposition, and in another school a shot whizzed past him one day while he was hearing a class recite, fired by some one outside, but by whom it was never known.

After studying again for a while at Fisk, he took charge of a school eight miles from Nashville. His habit at this time was to walk home on Friday night to attend the meeting of the students' literary society, of which he was a member, work at his tailor's trade all day on Saturday, and walk back on Sunday morning that he might be on hand to conduct th: Sabbath-school in his school-house. He was one of the original Jubilee Singers, and continued with the company until its return from its first visit to Great Britain, when he resumed his studies at Nashville. During the absence of the Singers on their second trip abroad he died of consumption ; the first death among those who have at any time been members of the Jubilee Singers' company.

ISAAC P. DICKERSON was born in Wytheville, Virginia. One of the first things he remembers was the sale of his father to a slave trader. When five years old he lost his mother, who was also a slave, by death. After emancipation, he went to Chattanooga, Tennessee, where he worked at anything he could find to do. Part of the time he attended an American Missionary Association school, and when sufficiently advanced in his studies began teaching school himself. But he failed to get his pay, and when he went to Fisk University the next year he was obliged to make economy one of his principal studies. He was very fond of music, and in the cantata of " Esther," in which so many of the Jubilee Singers made their *début*, he sang the part of Haman. When the Singers returned to America, in 1874, he remained in Edinburgh to pursue studies preparatory to entering the ministry. In 1878 he began evangelistic labors in France — work for which his connection with the Singers had in some respects given him a special training.

JUBILEE SONGS.

PREFACE TO THE MUSIC.

IN giving these melodies to the world in a tangible form, it seems desirable to say a few words about them as judged from a musical standpoint. It is certain that the critic stands completely disarmed in their presence. He must not only recognize their immense power over audiences which include many people of the highest culture, but, if he be not thoroughly encased in prejudice, he must yield a tribute of admiration on his own part, and acknowledge that these songs touch a chord which the most consummate art fails to reach. Something of this result is doubtless due to the singers as well as to their melodies. The excellent rendering of the Jubilee Band is made more effective and the interest is intensified by the comparison of their former state of slavery and degradation with the present prospects and hopes of their race, which crowd upon every listener's mind during the singing of their songs. Yet the power is chiefly in the songs themselves, and hence a brief analysis of them will be of interest.

Their origin is unique. They are never "composed" after the manner of ordinary music, but spring into life, ready-made, from the white heat of religious fervor during some protracted meeting in church or camp. They come from no musical cultivation whatever, but are the simple, ecstatic utterances of wholly untutored minds. From so unpromising a source we could reasonably expect only such a mass of crudities as would be unendurable to the cultivated ear. On the contrary, however, the cultivated listener confesses to a new charm, and to a power never before felt, at least in its kind. What can we infer from this but that the child-like, receptive minds of these unfortunates were wrought upon with a true inspiration, and that this gift was bestowed upon them by an ever-watchful Father, to quicken the pulses of life, and to keep them from the state of hopeless apathy into which they were in danger of falling.

A technical analysis of these melodies shows some interesting facts. The first peculiarity that strikes the attention is in the rhythm. This is often complicated, and sometimes strikingly original. But although so new and strange, it is most remarkable that these effects are so extremely satisfactory. We see few cases of what theorists call *mis-form*, although the student of musical composition is likely to fall into that error long after he has mastered the leading principles of the art.

Another noticeable feature of the songs is the rare occurrence of triple time, or three-part measure among them. The reason for this is doubtless to be found in the beating of the foot and the swaying of the body which are such frequent accompaniments of the singing. These motions are in even measure, and in perfect time; and so it will be found that, however broken and seemingly irregular the movement of the music, it is always capable of the most exact measurement. In other words, its irregularities invariably conform to the "higher law" of the perfect rhythmic flow.

It is a coincidence worthy of note that more than half the melodies in this connection are in the same scale as that in which Scottish music in written; that is, with the fourth and seventh tones omitted. The fact that the music of the ancient Greeks is also said to have been written in this scale suggests an interesting inquiry as to whether it may not be a peculiar language of nature, or a simpler alphabet than the ordinary. diatonic scale, in which the uncultivated mind finds its easiest expression.

THEO. F. SEWARD.

INDEX TO MUSIC.

JUBILEE SONGS.

I⊤ will be observed that in most of these songs the first strain is of the nature of a chorus or refrain, which is to be sung after each verse. The return to this chorus should be made without breaking the time.

In some of the verses the syllables do not correspond exactly to the notes in the music. The adaptation is so easy that it was thought best to leave it to the skill of the singer rather than to confuse the eye by too many notes. The music is in each case carefully adapted to the first verse. Whatever changes may be necessary in singing the remaining verses will be found to involve no difficulty.

No. 1.

Nobody knows the Trouble I see, Lord!

No-bo-dy knows the trouble I see, Lord, No-bo-dy knows the

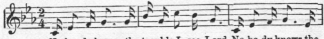

trou-ble I see, No-bo-dy knows the trouble I see, Lord,

FINE.

No-bo-dy knows like Je-sus. 1. Broth-ers, will you

pray for me, Brothers, will you pray for me, Brothers, will you

D. C.

pray for me, And help me to drive old Sa-tan a-way.

2. Sisters, will you pray for me, &c.
3. Mothers, will you pray for me, &c.
4. Preachers, will you pray for me, &c.

125

Swing low, sweet char-i-ot, Com-ing for to car-ry me home,

Swing low, sweet char-i-ot, Com-ing for to car-ry me home.

FINE.

1. I looked o - ver Jor - dan, and what did I see,
2. If you get there be - fore I do,
3. The bright - est day that ev - er I saw,
4. I'm some - times up and some - times down,

Com-ing for to car - ry me home? A band of an - gels
Com-ing for to car - ry me home, Tell all my friends I'm
Com-ing for to car - ry me home, When Je - sus wash'd my
Com-ing for to car - ry me home, But still my soul feels

D. C.

com-ing af - ter me, Com-ing for to car - ry me home.
com - ing too, Com-ing for to car - ry me home.
sins a - way, Com-ing for to car - ry me home.
heaven - ly bound, Com-ing for to car - ry me home.

126

Room Enough.

1. Oh, brothers, don't stay a - way, Brothers, don't stay a - way,

Broth-ers, don't stay a - way, Don't stay a - way.

Chorus.

For my Lord says there's room e-nough, Room e - nough in the

Heav'ns for you, My Lord says there's room enough, Don't stay away.

2 Oh, mourners, don't stay away.
   Cho.—For the Bible says there's room enough, &c.

3 Oh sinners, don't stay away.
   Cho.—For the angel says there's room enough, &c.

4 Oh, children, don't stay away.
   Cho.—For Jesus says there's room enough, &c.

* The peculiar accent here makes the words sound thus : "rooma nough."

No. 4. O Redeemed.

CHORUS.

O redeemed, re-deemed, I'm washed in the blood of the Lamb, O redeemed, re-deemed, I'm wash'd in the blood of the Lamb.

FINE.

1. Al-though you see me going a-long so, Washed in the
2. When I was a mourner just like you, Washed in the
3. Re-li-gion's like a bloom-ing rose, Washed in the

blood of the Lamb, I have my tri-als here be-low,
blood of the Lamb, I mourned and prayed till I got through,
blood of the Lamb, As none but those that feel it knows,

D. S.

Washed in the blood of the Lamb. O redeemed, re-deemed,

* Attention is called to this characteristic manner of connecting the last strain
with the chorus in the D. C.

From every Graveyard.

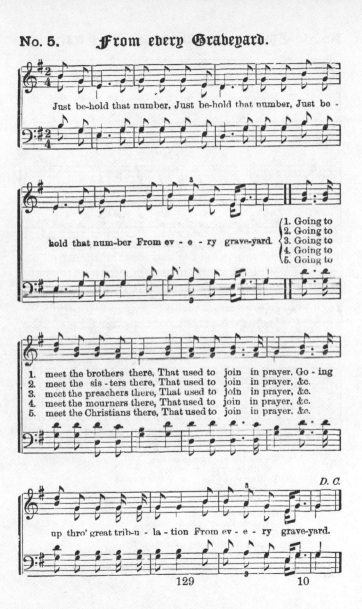

Just be-hold that number, Just be-hold that number, Just be - hold that num-ber From ev - e - ry grave-yard.

1. Going to
2. Going to
3. Going to
4. Going to
5. Going to

1. meet the brothers there, That used to join in prayer, Go - ing
2. meet the sis - ters there, That used to join in prayer, &c.
3. meet the preachers there, That used to join in prayer, &c.
4. meet the mourners there, That used to join in prayer, &c.
5. meet the Christians there, That used to join in prayer, &c.

D. C.

up thro' great trib-u - la - tion From ev - e - ry grave-yard.

10

No. 6. Children, we all shall be Free.

Chil-dren, we all shall be free, Chil-dren, we all shall be free, Children, we all shall be free, When the Lord shall appear.

1. We want no cowards in our band, That from their colors fly, We call for val-iant-heart-ed men, That are not a-fraid to die.

D. C.

2. We see the pilgrim as he lies,
With glory in his soul;
To Heaven he lifts his longing eyes,
And bids this world adieu.
CHO.—Children, we all shall be free, &c.

3. Give ease to the sick, give sight to the blind,
Enable the cripple to walk;
He'll raise the dead from under the earth,
And give them permission to fly.
CHO.—Children, we all shall be free, &c.

* The words, "On Jordan's stormy banks I stand," are sometimes sung to this strain.

Roll, Jordan, Roll.

Roll, Jordan, roll, roll, Jordan, roll, I want to go to

Roll, . . .

hea-ven when I die, To hear Jor-dan roll.

1. Oh, brothers, you ought t'have been there, Yes, my Lord! A

D.C.

sit-ting in the Kingdom, To hear Jor-dan roll.

2. Oh, preachers, you ought t'have been there, &c.
3. Oh, sinners, you ought, &c.
4. Oh, mourners, you ought, &c.
5. Oh, seekers, you ought, &c.
6. Oh, mothers, you ought, &c.
7. Oh, sisters, you ought, &c.

131

No. 8. Turn back Pharaoh's Army.

SOLO. *Moderato.*

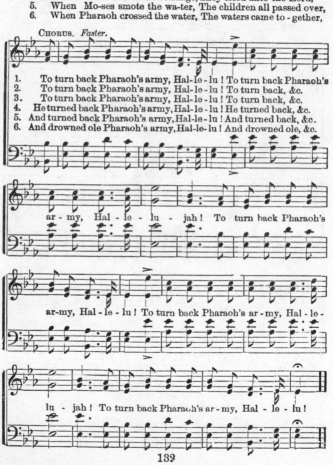

1. Gwine to write to Mas-sa Je-sus, To send some valiant soldier,
2. If you want your souls converted, You'd better be a-praying,
3. You say you are a soldier, Fighting for your Saviour,
4. When the children were in bondage, They cried unto the Lord,
5. When Mo-ses smote the wa-ter, The children all passed over,
6. When Pharaoh crossed the water, The waters came to-gether,

CHORUS. *Faster.*

1. To turn back Pharaoh's army, Hal-le-lu! To turn back Pharaoh's
2. To turn back Pharaoh's army, Hal-le-lu! To turn back, &c.
3. To turn back Pharaoh's army, Hal-le-lu! To turn back, &c.
4. He turned back Pharaoh's army, Hal-le-lu! He turned back, &c.
5. And turned back Pharaoh's army, Hal-le-lu! And turned back, &c.
6. And drowned ole Pharaoh's army, Hal-le-lu! And drowned ole, &c.

ar-my, Hal-le-lu-jah! To turn back Pharaoh's

ar-my, Hal-le-lu! To turn back Pharaoh's ar-my, Hal-le-

lu-jah! To turn back Pharaoh's ar-my, Hal-le-lu!

I'm a Rolling.

I'm a roll-ing, I'm a roll-ing, I'm a roll-ing thro' an un-friend-ly world, I'm a roll-ing, I'm a roll-ing thro' an un-friend-ly world.

1. O brothers, wont you help me,
2. O sis-ters, wont you help me,
3. O preachers, wont you help me,

O brothers, wont you help me to pray? O brothers, wont you
O sis-ters, wont you help me to pray? O sis-ters, &c.
O preachers, wont you help me to fight? O preachers, &c.

D. C.

help me, Wont you help me in the service of the Lord?*

* Return to the beginning in exact time.

Sung in Unison.

Did-n't my Lord de-liv-er Dan - iel, D'liver

Dan - iel, d'liver Dan-iel, Did-u't my Lord de - liv - er

1st Verse.

Dan - iel, And why not a ev-e-ry man? He de-

liv-er'd Dan-iel from the li-on's den, Jo-nah from the

bel-ly of the whale, And the He-brew children from the

fie-ry fur-nace, And why not ev-e-ry man?

Did-n't my Lord de-liv-er Dan - iel. D'liver

Dan-iel, d'liver Dan-iel, Did-n't my Lord de-liv-er

* Go on without pause, leaving out two beats of the measure.

134

Dan - iel, And why not a ev - e - ry man?

2D VERSE.

The moon run down in a purple-stream, The sun for - bear to

D. C. "Didn't my Lord."

shine, And ev - e - ry star dis-ap-pear, King Jesus shall be mine.

3D VERSE.

The wind blows East, and the wind blows West, It

blows like the judg-ment day, And ev - ery poor soul that

D. C. "Didn't my Lord."

nev - er did pray, 'll be glad to pray that day.

4TH VERSE.

I set my foot on the Gos - pel ship, And the

ship it be - gin to sail, It land-ed me o - ver on

D. C. "Didn't my Lord."

Ca-naan's shore, And I'll nev - er come back a - ny more.

No. 11. I'll hear the Trumpet Sound.

You may bur-y me in the East, You may bur-y me in the West; But I'll hear the trumpet sound In that morning.

In that morn-ing, my Lord, How I long to go, For to hear the trum-pet sound, In that morn - ing.

2. Father Gabriel in that day,
He'll take wings and fly away,
For to hear the trumpet sound
In that morning.
You may bury him in the East,
You may bury him in the West;
But he'll take the trumpet sound,
In that morning.
 Cho.—In that morning, &c.

3. Good old christians in that day,
They'll take wings and fly away,&c.
 Cho.—In that morning, &c.

4. Good old preachers in that day,
They'll take wings and fly away,&c.
 Cho.—In that morning, &c.

5. In that dreadful Judgment day,
I'll take wings and fly away, &c.
 Cho.—In that morning, &c.

* Repeat the music of the first strain for all the verses but the first.

No. 12. Rise, Mourners.*

1. Rise, mourners, rise, mourners, O can't you rise and
2. Rise, seekers, rise, seekers, O can't you rise, &c.
3. Rise, sinners, rise, sinners, O can't you rise, &c.
4. Rise, brothers, rise, brothers, O can't you rise, &c.

FINE.

tell, What the Lord has done for you. Yes, he's taken my feet out of the

D. C.

mi - ry clay, And he's placed them on the right side of my Father.

* This hymn is sung with great unction while "seekers" are going forward to the altar.

No. 13. I've just come from the Fountain.

1. I've just come from the fountain, I've just come from the
2. Been drinking from the fountain, Been drinking, &c.

fountain, Lord! I've just come from the fountain, His name's so

CHORUS.

sweet. O brothers, I love Je-sus, O brothers, I love

D. C.

Je-sus. O brothers, I love Je-sus, His name's so sweet.

3. I found free grace at the fountain,
   I found free grace, &c.
     Cho.—O preachers, I love Jesus, &c.

4. My soul's set free at the fountain,
   My soul's set free, &c.
     Cho.—O sinners, I love Jesus, &c.

* The Tenors usually sing the melody from this point.

No. 14. Gwine to ride up in the Chariot.

Solo. Chorus.

1. Gwine to ride up in the chariot, Soon-er in the morning.

Solo. Chorus.

Ride up in the cha-riot, Soon-er in the morn-ing.

Solo. Chorus.

Ride up in the cha-riot, Soon-er in the morning, And I

hope I'll join the band. O Lord, have mer-cy on me,

O Lord, have mer-cy on me; O Lord, have

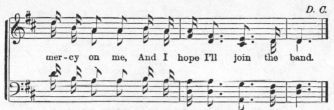

mer-cy on me, And I hope I'll join the band.

2. Gwine to meet my brother there, Sooner, &c.
   Cho.—O Lord, have mercy, &c.

3. Gwine to chatter with the Angels, Sooner, &c.
   Cho.—O Lord, have mercy, &c.

4. Gwine to meet my massa Jesus, Sooner, &c.
   Cho.—O Lord, have mercy, &c.

5. Gwine to walk and talk with Jesus, Sooner, &c.
   Cho.—O Lord, have mercy, &c.

No. 15. We'll die in the Field.

UNISON.

1. O what do you say, seekers, O what do you say, seekers; O what do you say, seekers, A-bout the Gospel war?

And I will die in the field, Will die in the field;

Will die in the field, I'm on my jour-ney home.

2. O what do you say, brothers, &c.
3. O what do you say, christians, &c.
4. O what do you say, preachers, &c.

139

No. 16. Children, you'll be called on.

1. Chil-dren, you'll be called on To march in the field of
2. Preachers, you'll be called on To march in the field, &c.
3. Sin-ners, you'll be called on To march in the field, &c.
4. Seek-ers, you'll be called on To march in the field, &c.
5. Christians, you'll be called on To march in the field, &c.

bat - tle, When this war - fare'll be end - ed, Hal - le - lu.

CHORUS.

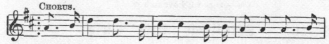

When this war - fare'll be end-ed, I'm a sol-dier of the

. C.

ju - bi-lee, This warfare'll be ended, I'm a soldier of the cross.

No. 17. Give me Jesus.

1. O when I come to die, O when I come to die, O
2. In the morning when I rise, In the morning when I rise, &c.
3. Dark midnight was my cry, Dark midnight was my cry, &c.
4. I heard the mourner say, I heard the mourner say, &c.

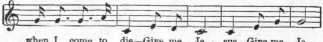

when I come to die—Give me Je - sus, Give me Je

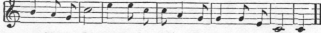

sus, Give me Je - sus, You may have all this world, Give me Je-sus.

140

No. 18. The Rocks and the Mountains.

Oh, the rocks and the mountains shall all flee a-way, And you shall have a new hid-ing-place that day.

1. Seek-er, seek-er, give up your heart to God, And you shall have a new hid-ing-place that day.

D. C.

2. Doubter, doubter, give up your heart to God,
   And you shall have a new hiding-place that day.
       Oh, the rocks, &c.

3. Mourner, mourner, give up your heart to God, &c.

4. Sinner, sinner, give up your heart to God, &c.

5. Sister, sister, give up your heart to God, &c.

6. Mother, mother, give up your heart to God, &c.

7. Children, children, give up your heart to God, &c.

141

Go down, Moses.

1. When Is-rael was in E-gypt's land: Let my people go,
Oppress'd so hard they could not stand, Let my peo-ple go.
Go down, Mo-ses, Way down in E-gypt land,
Tell ole Pha-roh. Let my peo-ple go.

2. Thus saith the Lord, bold Moses said,
   Let my people go ;
   If not I'll smite your first-born dead,
   Let my people go.
   Go down, Moses, &c.

3. No more shall they in bondage toil,
   Let my people go ;
   Let them come out with Egypt's spoil,
   Let my people go.
   Go down, Moses, &c.

142

4. When Israel out of Egypt came,
   Let my people go;
   And left the proud oppressive land,
   Let my people go.
   Go down, Moses, &c.

5. O, 'twas a dark and dismal night,
   Let my people go;
   When Moses led the Israelites.
   Let my people go.
   Go down, Moses, &c.

6. 'Twas good old Moses and Aaron, too,
   Let my people go;
   'Twas they that led the armies through,
   Let my people go.
   Go down, Moses, &c.

7. The Lord told Moses what to do.
   Let my people go;
   To lead the children of Israel through,
   Let my people go.
   Go down, Moses, &c.

8. O come along, Moses, you'll not get lost,
   Let my people go;
   Stretch out your rod and come across,
   Let my people go.
   Go down, Moses, &c.

9. As Israel stood by the water side,
   Let my people go;
   A' the command of God it did divide,
   Let my people go.
   Go down, Moses, &c.

10. When they had reached the other shore,
    Let my people go;
    They sang a song of triumph o'er.
    Let my people go.
    Go down, Moses, &c.

11. Pharaoh said he would go across.
    Let my people go;
    But Pharaoh and his host were lost.
    Let my people go.
    Go down, Moses, &c.

12. O, Moses, the cloud shall cleave the way,
    Let my people go;
    A fire by night, a shade by day,
    Let my people go.
    Go down, Moses, &c.

13. You'll not get lost in the wilderness,
    Let my people go;
    With a lighted candle in your breast,
    Let my people go.
    Go down, Moses, &c.

14. Jordan shall stand up like a wall,
    Let my people go;
    And the walls of Jericho shall fall.
    Let my people go.
    Go down, Moses, &c.

15. Your foes shall not before you stand
    Let my people go;
    And you'll possess fair Canaan's land,
    Let my people go.
    Go down, Moses, &c.

16. 'Twas just about in harvest time.
    Let my people go;
    When Joshua led his host divine.
    Let my people go.
    Go down, Moses, &c.

17. O let us all from bondage flee,
    Let my people go;
    And let us all in Christ be free,
    Let my people go.
    Go down, Moses, &c.

18. We need not always weep and moan,
    Let my people go;
    And wear these slavery chains forlorn.
    Let my people go.
    Go down, Moses, &c.

19. This world's a wilderness of woe,
    Let my people go;
    O, let us on to Canaan go,
    Let my people go.
    Go down, Moses, &c.

20. What a beautiful morning that will be,
    Let my people go;
    When time breaks up in eternity.
    Let my people go.
    Go down, Moses, &c.

21. O bretheren, bretheren, you'd better be engaged,
    Let my people go;
    For the devil he's out on a big rampage,
    Let my people go.
    Go down, Moses, &c.

22. The Devil he thought he had me fast,
    Let my people go;
    But I thought I'd break his chains at last,
    Let my people go.
    Go down, Moses, &c.

23. O take yer shoes from off yer feet,
    Let my people go;
    And walk into the golden street,
    Let my people go.
    Go down, Moses, &c.

24. I'll tell you what I likes de best,
    Let my people go;
    It is the shouting Methodist,
    Let my people go.
    Go down, Moses, &c.

25. I do believe without a doubt,
    Let my people go;
    That a Christian has the right to shout.
    Let my people go.
    Go down, Moses, &c.

143

Been a Listening.

Been a lis - ten - ing all the night long, Been a

lis - ten - ing all the night long, Been a

FINE.

lis - ten - ing all the night long, To hear some sinner pray.

1. Some say that John the Baptist was nothing but a Jew, But the
2. Go read the third of Matthew, And read the chapter thro', It

D. C. "Been a listening."

Ho - ly Bi - ble tells us he was a preach-er too.
is the guide for Christians, and tells them what to do

144

Keep me from sinking Down.

Oh, Lord, Oh, my Lord! Oh, my good Lord! Keep

me from sink-ing down.

1. I tell you what I
2. I look up yonder, and

mean to do; Keep me from sink-ing down: I
what do I see; Keep me from sink-ing down: I

mean to go to heav-en too; Keep me from sinking down.
see the angels beckoning to me; Keep me from sinking down.

3. When I was a mourner just like you;
 Keep me from sinking down:
I mourned and mourned till I got through;
 Keep me from sinking down.
  Oh, Lord, &c.

4. I bless the Lord I'm gwine to die;
 Keep me from sinking down:
I'm gwine to judgment by-and-by;
 Keep me from sinking down.
  Oh, Lord, &c.

11

No. 22. I'm a trav'ling to the Grave.

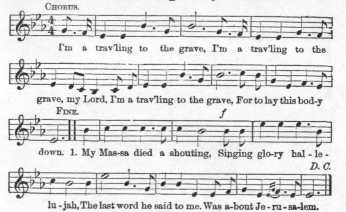

CHORUS.

I'm a trav'ling to the grave, I'm a trav'ling to the grave, my Lord, I'm a trav'ling to the grave, For to lay this bod-y down. 1. My Mas-sa died a shouting, Singing glo-ry hal - le - lu - jah, The last word he said to me. Was a-bout Je - ru - sa-lem.

2. My missis died a shouting, &c.
3. My brother died a shouting, &c.
4. My sister died a shouting, &c.

No. 23. Many Thousand Gone.

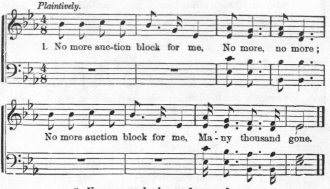

Plaintively.

1. No more auc-tion block for me, No more, no more; No more auction block for me, Ma-ny thousand gone.

2. No more peck o' corn for me, &c.
3. No more driver's lash for me, &c.
4. No more pint o' salt for me, &c.
5. No more hundred lash for me, &c.
6. No more mistress' call for me, &c.

146

Steal Away.

Steal a - way, steal a - way, steal a - way to Je - sus!

Steal a-way, steal a-way home, I hain't got long to stay here.

1. My Lord calls me, He calls me by the thunder; The
2. Green trees are bending, Poor sin-ners stand trembling; The, &c

trumpet sounds it in my soul: I hain't got long to stay here.

3. My Lord calls me,
He calls me by the lightning;
The trumpet sounds it in my soul:
I hain't got long to stay here.
Cho.—Steal away, &c.

4. Tombstones are bursting,
Poor sinners are trembling;
The trumpet sounds it in my soul:
I hain't got long to stay here.
Cho.—Steal away, &c.

11 *

He's the Lord of Lords.

Why, He's the Lord of lords, And the King of kings, Why

Je - sus Christ is the first and the last, No one can work like Him.

1. I will not let you go, my Lord; No one can work like Him, Un-

til you come and bless my soul. No one can work like Him.

2. For Paul and Silas bound in jail,
   No one can work like Him;
   The Christians prayed both night and day,
   No one can work like Him.
       Cho.—Why, He's the Lord of lords, &c.

3. I wish those mourners would believe.
   No one can work like Him,
   That Jesus is ready to receive,
   No one can work like Him.
       Cho.—Why, He's the Lord of lords, &c

Judgment, Judgment, Judgment day is roll-ing around; Judgment, Judgment, O how I long to go. 1. I've a good old mother in the heav-en, my Lord How I long to go there too, I've a good old mother in the heaven, my Lord, O how I long to go.

2. There's no backsliding in the heaven, my Lord,
   How I long to go there too,
   There's no backsliding in the heaven, my Lord,
   O how I long to go.
   Cho.—Judgment, &c.

3. King Jesus sitting in the heaven, my Lord,
   How I long to go there too,
   King Jesus sitting in the heaven, my Lord,
   O how I long to go.
   Cho.—Judgment, &c.

4. There's a big camp meeting in the heaven, my Lord,
   How I long to go there too,
   There's a big camp meeting in the heaven, my Lord,
   O how I long to go.
   Cho.—Judgment, &c.

The Gospel Train.

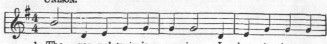

UNISON.

1. The gos-pel train is com-ing, I hear it just at
2. I hear the bell and whis-tle, The com-ing round the
3. No sig-nal for an-oth-er train To fol-low on the

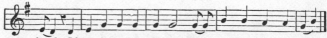

hand, I hear the car wheels moving, And rumbling thro' the land.
curve; She's playing all her steam and pow'r And straining every nerve.
line, O, sinner, you're forever lost, If once you're left be-hind.

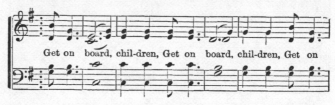

Get on board, chil-dren, Get on board, chil-dren, Get on

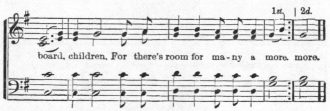

1st. | 2d.

board, children, For there's room for ma-ny a more. more.

4. This is the Christian banner,
  The motto's new and old,
Salvation and Repentance
  Are burnished there in gold.
    Cho.—Get on board, children, &c.

5. She's nearing now the station,
  O, sinner, don't be vain,
But come and get your ticket,
  And be ready for the train.
    Cho.—Get on board, children, &c.

6. The fare is cheap and all can go,
  The rich and poor are there,
No second-class on board the train,
  No difference in the fare.
    Cho.—Get on board, children, &c.

7. There's Moses, Noah and Abraham,
   And all the prophets, too,
   Our friends in Christ are all on board,
   O, what a heavenly crew.
      Cho.—Get on board, children, &c.

8. We soon shall reach the station,
   O, how we then shall sing,
   With all the heavenly army,
   We'll make the welkin ring,
      Cho.—Get on board, children, &c.

9. We'll shout o'er all our sorrows,
   And sing forever more,
   With Christ and all his army,
   On that celestial shore.
      Cho.—Get on board, children, &c.

No. 28. Shine, Shine.

Shine, shine, I'll meet you in the morning, Shine, shine, I'll
meet you in the morning, Shine, shine, I'll meet you in the morning,
Oh! my soul's going to shine, shine, Oh! my soul's going to shine, shine.

1. I'm going to sit at the wel-come-ta-ble, I'm going to sit at the
wel-come ta-ble, I'm going to sit at the wel-come ta-ble,

D. C.

Oh! my soul's going to shine, shine, Oh! my soul's going to shine, shine.

2. I'm going to tell God about my trial, &c.
   Oh! my soul's going to shine, &c.
      Cho.—Shine, shine, &c.

3. I'm going to walk all about that city, &c.
   Oh! my soul's going to shine, &c.
      Cho.—Shine, shine, &c.

Old Ship of Zion.

Repeat twice for first verse

1. { What ship is that a sail-ing, Hal-le-lu-
     'Tis the old ship of Zi-on, Hal-le-lu-
     Do you think that she is a-ble, Hal-le-lu-

jah, What ship is that a sail-ing, Hal-le-lu.
jah, 'Tis the old ship of Zi-on, Hal-le-lu.
jah, Do you think that she is a-ble, Hal-le-lu.

Do you think that she is a-ble, For to

car-ry us all.... home. O glo-ry, Hal-le-lu.

In singing the last two verses the music is not to be repeated.

2. She has landed many a thousand, Hallelujah,
   She has landed many a thousand, Hallelu,
   She has landed many a thousand,
   And will land as many a more. Oh glory, Hallelu.

3. She is loaded down with angels, Hallelujah,
   She is loaded down with angels, Hallelu,
   And King Jesus is the Captain,
   And he'll carry us all home. Oh glory, Hallelu.

152

1. In the riv - er of Jor-dan John baptized, How I long to be bap-tized; In the riv - er of Jor-dan John bap-tized, To the dy - ing Lamb. Pray on, pray on, pray on, ye mourning souls, Pray on, pray on, un - to the dy-ing Lamb.

2. We baptize all that come by faith,
    How I long to be baptized ;
   We baptize all that come by faith,
    To the dying Lamb.
     Cho.—Pray on, &c.

3. Here's another one come to be baptized,
    How I long to be baptized ;
   Here's another one come to be baptized,
    To the dying Lamb
     Cho.—Pray on, &c.

Oh! stand the storm, it won't be long, We'll anchor by-and-by,

Stand the storm, it won't be long, We'll an-chor by - and-by.

1. My ship is on the o - cean, We'll anchor by-and-by, My

ship is on the o - cean, We'll an-chor by - and-by.

2. She's making for the kingdom,
   We'll anchor, &c.

3. I've a mother in the kingdom,
   We'll anchor, &c.

154

I'm so Glad.

I'm so glad, I'm so glad, I'm so glad there's no dy-ing there. 1. I'll tell you how I found the Lord, No dy-ing there. With a hung down head and ach-ing heart, No dy-ing there

D. C.

2. I hope I'll meet my brother there,
   No dying there,
That used to join with me in prayer,
   No dying there.
   Cho.—I'm so glad, &c.

3. I hope I'll meet the preacher there,
   No dying there,
That used to join with me in prayer,
   No dying there.
   Cho.—I'm so glad, &c.

No. 33. Come, let us all go Down.

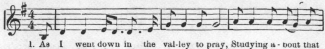

1. As I went down in the val-ley to pray, Studying a-bout that
2. I think I hear the sinner say, Come, let's go in the val-
3. I think I hear the mourner say, Come, let's go in the val-

good old way; You shall wear the starry crown, Good Lord, show me the way.
ley to pray; You shall wear the starry crown, Good Lord, show me the way.
ley to pray; You shall wear the starry crown, Good Lord, show me the way.

By - and - by we'll all go down, all go down, all go down,

By - and-by we'll all go down, Down in the val-ley to pray.

No. 34. Zion's Children.

Oh! Zi - on's children com-ing a - long, Com-ing a - long,

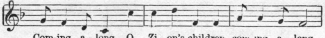

Com-ing a - long, O Zi - on's children com-ing a - long,

Talk - ing a - bout the wel - come day. {
1. I
2. Oh!
3. I

hail my moth-er in the morn -ing, Com-ing a - long,
don't you want to live up yon - der, Com-ing, &c.
think they are might-y hap - py, Com-ing, &c.

156

com - ing a - long, I hail my moth - er in the

D. C.

morn - ing, Talk-ing a - bout the wel - come day.

No. 35. **Oh! Holy Lord.**

Oh! ho - ly Lord! Oh! ho - ly Lord!

Oh! ho - ly Lord! Done with the sin and

sor - row. 1. Oh! rise up chil - dren, get your crown,

Done with the sin and sor - row, And by your Sav-iour's

D. C.

side sit down, Done with the sin and sor = row.

2. What a glorious morning that will be,
   Done with the sin and sorrow;
   Our friends and Jesus we will see,
   Done with the sin and sorrow.—*Cho.*

3. Oh shout, you Christians, you're gaining **ground,**
   Done with the sin and sorrow;
   We'll shout old Satan's kingdom down,
   Done with the sin and sorrow.—*Cho.*

4. I soon shall reach that golden shore,
   Done with the sin and sorrow;
   And sing the songs we sang before,
   Done with the sin and sorrow.—*Cho.*

Oh! this old time re - li - gion, This old time re - li - gion, This old time re - li - gion, It is good e - nough for me.

1. It is good for the mourner, It is good for the mourner, It is good for the mourner, It is good e - nough for me.

2. It will carry you home to heaven,
   It will carry you home to heaven,
   It will carry you home to heaven,
   It is good enough for me.
      Cho.—Oh, this old time religion, &c.

3. It brought me out of bondage, &c.
      Cho.—Oh, this old time religion, &c.

4. It is good when you are in trouble, &c.
      Cho.—Oh, this old time religion, &c.

The Ten Virgins.

1. Five of them were wise when the bride-groom came.

Five of them were wise when the bride-groom came.

Repeat. pp

O Zi-on, O Zi-on, O Zi-on, when the bridegroom came.

2. Five of them were foolish when the bridegroom came,
   Five of them were foolish when the bridegroom came.
       Cho.—O Zion, &c.

3. The wise they took oil when the bridegroom came,
   The wise they took oil when the bridegroom came.
       Cho.—O Zion, &c.

4. The foolish took no oil when the bridegroom came,
   The foolish took no oil when the bridegroom came.
       Cho.—O Zion, &c.

5. The foolish they kept knocking when the bridegroom came,
   The foolish they kept knocking when the bridegroom came.
       Cho.—O Zion, &c.

6. Depart, I never knew you, said the bridegroom, then,
   Depart, I never knew you, said the bridegroom, then.
       Cho.—O Zion, &c.

He Arose.

Slowly.

1. The Jews killed poor Jesus, The Jews killed poor Jesus, The Jews killed poor Je - sus, And laid him in a tomb.

He a - rose,........ He a - rose,........ He a - rose, ... He a - rose and went to heav-en in a cloud.

Repeat. pp

2. Then down came an angel,
Then down came an angel,
Then down came an angel,
And rolled away the stone
Cho.—He arose, &c.

3. Then Mary she came weeping,
Then Mary she came weeping,
Then Mary she came weeping,
A looking for her Lord.
Cho.—He arose, &c.

Save me, Lord, Save. .

1. I called to my fa-ther, my fa-ther hearkened to me, And the last word I heard him say, was, Save me, Lord, save me.

And I wish that heav'n was a mine, And I hope that heav'n will a be mine, And I wish that heav'n was a mine, O save me, Lord, save me.

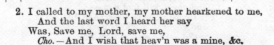

2. I called to my mother, my mother hearkened to me,
    And the last word I heard her say
Was, Save me, Lord, save me,
    Cho.—And I wish that heav'n was a mine, &c.

3. I called to my sister, my sister hearkened to me, &c.
    Cho.—And I wish that heav'n was a mine, &c.

4. I called to my brother, my brother hearkened to me, &c.
    Cho.—And I wish that heav'n was a mine, &c.

Just as you live, just so you die, And af-ter death,

Judg-ment will find you so. 1. O brethren, brethren,

watch and pray, Judg-ment will find you so, For

D. C.

Sa-tan's round you ev-'ry day, Judgment will find you so.

2. The tallest tree in paradise,
 Judgment will find you so ;
The Christian calls the tree of life,
 Judgment will find you so.
  Cho.—Just as you live, &c.

3. Oh ! Hallelujah to the Lamb,
 Judgment will find you so ;
The Lord is on the giving hand,
 Judgment will find you so.
  Cho.—Just as you live, &c.

No. 41. He's the Lily of the Valley.

He's the li - ly of the val - ley, Oh! my

Lord; He's the li - ly of the val - ley, Oh, my Lord;

1. King Je - sus in the cha - riot rides, Oh! my Lord; With

D. C.

four white hors - es side by side, Oh! my Lord.

2. What kind of shoes are those you wear,
    Oh! my Lord;
   That you can ride upon the air,
    Oh! my Lord.
      Cho.—He's the lily of the valley, &c.

3. These shoes I wear are gospel shoes,
    Oh! my Lord;
   And you can wear them if you choose,
    Oh! my Lord.
      Cho.—He's the lily of the valley, &c.

Prepare us.

Pre-pare me, Pre-pare me, Lord, Pre-pare me, When death shall shake this frame. 1. As I go down the stream of time, When death shall shake this frame, I'll leave this sin-ful world behind, When death shall shake this frame.

D. C.

2. The man that loves to serve the Lord,
   When death shall shake this frame ;
   He will receive his just reward,
   When death shall shake this frame.
   Cho.—Prepare me, &c.

3. Am I a soldier of the cross,
   When death shall shake this frame ;
   Or must I count this soul as lost,
   When death shall shake this frame.
   Cho.—Prepare me, &c.

4. My soul is bound for that bright land,
   When death shall shake this frame ;
   And there I'll meet that happy band,
   When death shall shake this frame.
   Cho.—Prepare me, &c.

No. 43.   My Ship is on the Ocean.

My ship is on the o-cean, My ship is on the o-cean, My

ship is on the o - cean, Poor sin - ner, fare - you - well.

1. I'm go - ing a - way to see the good old Dan-iel, I'm

D. C.

go - ing a - way To see my Lord.

2. I'm going to see the weeping Mary,
   I'm going away to see my Lord.
   Cho.—My ship, &c.

3. Oh! don't you want to live in that bright **glory**?
   Oh! don't you want to go to see my Lord?
   Cho.—My ship, &c.

March On.

1. Way o-ver in the E-gypt land, You shall gain the vic-to-ry, Way o-ver in the E-gypt land, You shall gain the day. March on, and you shall gain the vic-to-ry, March on, and you shall gain the day.

Repeat. pp

2. When Peter was preaching at the Pentecost,
   You shall gain the victory ;
   He was endowed with the Holy Ghost,
   You shall gain the day.
     Cho.—March on, &c.

3. When Peter was fishing in the sea,
   You shall gain the victory ;
   He dropped his net and followed **me**,
   You shall gain the day.
     Cho. March on, &c.

4. King Jesus on the mountain top,
   You shall gain the victory ;
   King Jesus speaks and the chariot **stops**,
   You shall gain the day.
     Cho.—March on, &c.

My Way's Cloudy.

Oh! breth-er-en, my way, my way's cloud-y, my way, Go send them an-gels down, Oh! broth-er-en, my way, my way's cloud-y, my way, Go send them an-gels down.

1. There's fire in the east and fire in the west, Send them angels down, And
2. Old Sa-tan's mad, and I am glad, Send them angels down, He
3. I'll tell you now as I told you before, Send them angels down, To
4. This is the year of Ju-bi-lee, Send them angels down, The

D. C.

fire a-mong the Meth-o-dist, O send them an-gels down.
missed the soul he thought he had, O send them an-gels down.
the promised land I'm bound to go, O send them an-gels down.
Lord has come and set us free, O send them an-gels down.

Ride on, King Jesus.

Ride on, King Je - sus, No man can a hin-der me,

Ride on, King Je - sus, No man can a hinder me.

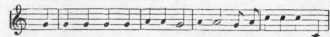

1. I was but young when I begun, No man can a hinder me, But

D. C.

now my race is almost done, No man can a hinder me.

2. King Jesus rides on a milk-white horse,
   No man can a hinder me ;
   The river of Jordan he did cross,
   No man can a hinder me.
   Cho.—Ride on, &c.

3. If you want to find your way to God,
   No man can a hinder me ;
   The gospel highway must be trod,
   No man can a hinder me.
   Cho.—Ride on, &c.

No. 47.

These are my Father's Children.

These are my Father's children, These are my Father's children,

These are my Father's chil-dren, All.... in one band.

1. And I soon shall be done with the troubles of the world.

168

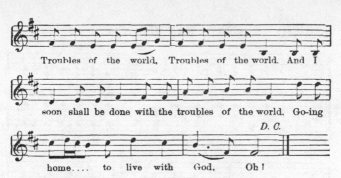

Troubles of the world, Troubles of the world. And I

soon shall be done with the troubles of the world. Go-ing

D. C.

home.... to live with God, Oh!

2. My brother's done with the troubles of the world, &c.
   Cho.—These are my Father's children, &c.

3. My sister's done with the troubles of the world, &c.
   Cho.—These are my Father's children. &c.

No. 48. Reign, Oh! Reign.

Reign, Oh! reign, O reign, my Sav-iour, Reign, Oh!

reign. O reign, my Lord. 1. Takes an hum-ble soul to

join us in the ser-vice of the Lord, Takes an

D. C.

hum-ble soul to join us in the ar-my.

2. Here's a sinner come to join us in the service of the Lord,
   Here's a sinner come to join us in the army.
      Cho.—Reign, Oh! reign, &c.

3. Oh! ain't you glad you've joined us in the service of the Lord;
   Oh! ain't you glad you've joined us in the army.
      Cho.—Reign, Oh! reign, &c.

Mary and Martha.

1. Ma-ry and a Martha's just gone 'long, Ma-ry and a Martha's
just gone 'long, Ma-ry and a Mar-tha's just gone 'long, To
ring those charming bells; Cry-ing free grace and dy-ing love,
Free grace and dy-ing love, Free grace and dy-ing love, To
ring those charming bells. Oh! way o-ver Jordan, Lord, Way o-ver

Jordan, Lord, Way over Jordan, Lord, To ring those charming bells.

2. The preacher and the elder's just gone 'long, &c.
   To ring those charming bells.
   Cho.—Crying, free grace, &c.

3. My father and mother's just gone 'long, &c.
   To ring those charming bells.
   Cho.—Crying, free grace, &c.

4. The Methodist and Baptist's just gone 'long, &c.
   To ring those charming bells.
   Cho.—Crying, free grace, &c.

No. 50. I ain't going to die no more.

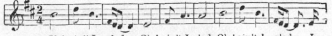

Oh! ain't I glad, Oh! ain't I glad, Oh! ain't I glad, I

ain't a going to die no more; 1. Going to meet those happy Christians

soon-er in the morn-ing, Soon-er in the morn-ing,

Soon-er in the morn-ing, Meet those hap-py Chris-tians

D. C.

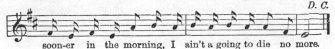

soon-er in the morning, I ain't a going to die no more.

2. Going shouting home to glory sooner in the morning, &c.
   Cho.—Oh! ain't I glad, &c.

3. Going to wear the starry crown sooner in the morning, &c.
   Cho.—Oh! ain't I glad, &c.

4. We'll sing our troubles over sooner in the morning, &c.
   Cho.—Oh! ain't I glad, &c.

No. 51. Getting Ready to Die.

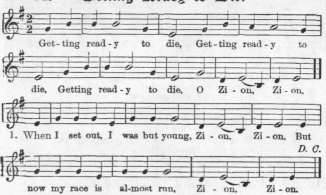

Get-ting read-y to die, Get-ting read-y to

die, Getting read-y to die, O Zi - on, Zi - on,

1. When I set out, I was but young, Zi - on, Zi - on, But

D. C.

now my race is al-most run, Zi - on, Zi - on.

2. Religion's like a blooming rose, Zion, Zion,
And none but those that feel it knows, Zion, Zion.
   Cho.—Getting ready to die, &c.

3. The Lord is waiting to receive, Zion, Zion,
If sinners only would believe, Zion, Zion.—*Chorus.*

4. All those who walk in Gospel shoes, Zion, Zion,
This faith in Christ they'll never lose, Zion, Zion.—*Chorus.*

No. 52. The General Roll.

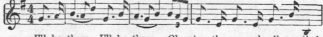

I'll be there, I'll be there, Oh when the general roll is called,

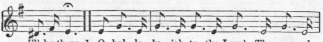

I'll be there. 1. O hal - le - lu - jah to the Lamb, The general
           2. Old Sa - tan told me not to pray, The general

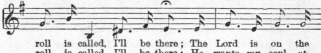

roll is called, I'll be there; The Lord is on the
roll is called, I'll be there; He wants my soul at

D. C.

giv-ing hand, The gen - eral roll is called, I'll be there.
Judgment Day, The gen - eral roll is called, I'll be there.

172

No. 53. I'm Troubled in Mind.

[The person who furnished this song (Mrs. Brown of Nashville, formerly a slave), stated that she first heard it from her old father when she was a child. After he had been whipped he always went and sat upon a certain log near his cabin, and with the tears streaming down his cheeks, sang this song with so much pathos that few could listen without weeping from sympathy : and even his cruel oppressors were not wholly unmoved.]

I'm troubled, I'm troubled, I'm troubled in mind, If Jesus don't

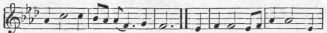

help me, I sure-ly will die. 1. O Je-sus, my Saviour, on

D. C.

thee I'll depend, When troubles are near me, you'll be my true friend.

2. When ladened with trouble and burdened with grief,
   To Jesus in secret I'll go for relief.
   Cho.—I'm troubled, &c.

3. In dark days of bondage to Jesus I prayed,
   To help me to bear it, and he gave me his aid.
   Cho.—I'm troubled, &c.

No. 54. I'm going to Live with Jesus.

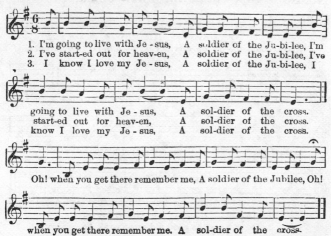

1. I'm going to live with Je - sus, A soldier of the Ju-bi-lee, I'm
2. I've start-ed out for heav-en, A soldier of the Ju-bi-lee, I've
3. I know I love my Je - sus, A soldier of the Ju-bi-lee, I

going to live with Je-sus, A sol-dier of the cross.
start-ed out for heav-en, A sol-dier of the cross.
know I love my Je-sus, A sol-dier of the cross.

Oh! when you get there remember me, A soldier of the Jubilee, Oh!

when you get there remember me. A sol-dier of the cross.

173

No. 55   **Oh! let me get up.**

1. Oh! just let me get up in the house of God, Just let me get up in the house of God, Just let me get up in the house of God, And I'll nev-er turn back a-ny more. No more, no more, why thank God al-might-y, No more, no more, I'll nev-er turn back a-ny more.

2. Oh! just let me get on my long white robe, &c
3. Oh! just let me get on my starry crown, &c.
4. Oh! just let me get on my golden shoes, &c.
5. Oh! the music in the heaven, and it sounds so sweet, &c.

No. 56.   **Go, chain the Lion down.**

Go, chain the li-on down, Go, chain the li-on down, Go, chain the li-on down, Be-fore the heav'n doors close. 1. Do you see that good old sis-ter, Come a wagging up the hill so slow, She

D. C.

wants to get to heav'n in due time, Be-fore the heav'n doors close.

2. Do you see the good old Christians? &c.
3. Do you see the good old preachers? &c.

When Moses smote the Water.

When Mo-ses smote the wa-ter, The chil-dren all passed o-ver, When Moses smote the wa-ter, The sea gave a-way.

1. O chil-dren ain't you glad You've left that sin-ful ar-my? O chil-dren ain't you glad The sea gave a-way?

D. C.

2. O Christians ain't you glad
   You've left that sinful army?
   O Christians ain't you glad
   The sea gave away?
       Cho.—When Moses smote, &c.

3. O brothers ain't you glad
   You've left that sinful army?
   O brothers ain't you glad
   The sea gave away?
       Cho.—When Moses smote, &c.

175

Oh! Sinner Man.

Oh! sin-ner, Oh! sin-ner man, Oh! sin-ner, Oh! which way are you go-ing? 1. Oh! come back, sinner, and don't go there, Which way are you going? For hell is deep, and dark des-pair. Oh! which way are you go-ing?

2. Though days be dark, and nights be long,
   Which way are you going?
   We'll shout and sing till we get home,
   Which way are you going?
   Cho.—Oh! sinner, &c.

3. 'Twas just about the break of day,
   Which way are you going?
   My sins forgiven and soul set free,
   Which way are you going?
   Cho.—Oh! sinner, &c.

My good Lord's been here.

My good Lord's been here, been here, been here,

My good Lord's been here, And he's blessed my soul and gone.

1. O brothers, where were you, broth-ers, where were you,

broth-ers, where were you When my good Lord was here?

2. O sinners, where were you, &c.
 Cho.—My good Lord's been here, &c.

3. O Christians, where were you, &c.
 Cho.—My good Lord's been here, &c.

4. O mourners, where were you, &c.
 Cho.—My good Lord's been here, &c.

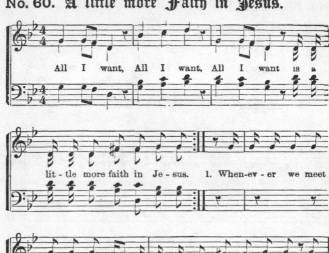

All I want, All I want, All I want is a

lit - tle more faith in Je - sus. 1. When-ev - er we meet

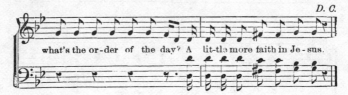

you here we say, A lit - tle more faith in Je - sus, Pray

D. C.

what's the or-der of the day? A lit-tle more faith in Je - sus.

2.

I tell you now as I told you before,
  A little more faith in Jesus,
To the promised land I'm bound to go,
  A little more faith in Jesus.
    Cho.—All I want, &c.

3.

Oh! Hallelujah to the Lamb,
  A little more faith in Jesus,
The Lord is on the giving hand,
  A little more faith in Jesus.
    Cho.—All I want, &c.

4.

I do believe without a doubt,
  A little more faith in Jesus,
That Christians have a right to shout,
  A little more faith in Jesus.
    Cho.—All I want, &c.

5.

Shout, you children, shout, you're free,
  A little more faith in Jesus,
For Christ has bought this liberty,
  A little more faith in Jesus.
    Cho.—All I want, &c.

No. 61. Did not old Pharaoh get lost?

1. I-saac a ran-som, while he lay Up-on an al-tar

bound, Mo-ses, an infant cast away, By Pharaoh's daughter found.

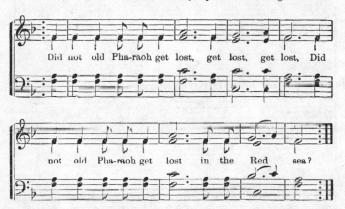

Did not old Pha-raoh get lost, get lost, get lost, Did

not old Pha-raoh get lost in the Red sea?

2. Joseph, by his false brethren sold,
   God raised above them all ;
   To Hannah's child the Lord foretold
   How Eli's house should fall.
   Cho.—Did not old Pharaoh, &c.

3. The Lord said unto Moses,
   Go unto Pharaoh now,
   For I have hardened Pharaoh's heart,
   To me he will not bow.
   Cho.—Did not old Pharaoh, &c.

4. Then Moses and Aaron,
   To Pharaoh did go,
   Thus says the God of Israel,
   Let my people go.
   Cho.—Did not old Pharaoh, &c.

5. Old Pharaoh said who is the Lord,
   That I should Him obey?
   His name it is Jehovah,
   For he hears his people pray,
   Cho.—Did not old Pharaoh, &c.

Then Moses numbered Israel,
   Through all the land abroad,
   Saying, children, do not murmur,
   But hear the word of God.
   Cho.—Did not old Pharaoh, &c.

7. Hark ! hear the children murmur,
   They cried aloud for bread,
   Down came the hidden manna,
   The hungry soldiers fed.
   Cho.—Did not old Pharaoh, &c.

8. Then Moses said to Israel,
   As they stood along the shore,
   Your enemies you see to-day,
   You will never see no more.
   Cho.—Did not old Pharaoh, &c.

9. Then down came raging Pharaoh,
   That you may plainly see,
   Old Pharaoh and his host,
   Got lost in the Red Sea.
   Cho.—Did not old Pharaoh, &c.

10. Then men, and women, and children
    To Moses they did flock ;
    They cried aloud for water,
    And Moses smote the rock.
    Cho.—Did not old Pharaoh, &c.

11. And the Lord spoke to Moses,
    From Sinai's smoking top,
    Saying, Moses, lead the people,
    Till I shall bid you stop.
    Cho.—Did not old Pharaoh, &c.

13 *

Wrestling Jacob.

1. Wrest-ling Ja-cob, Ja-cob, day is a-breaking,

Fine.

Wrest-ling Ja-cob, Ja-cob, I will not let thee go.

Let me go, Ja-cob. I will not let thee go.

Let me go, Ja-cob. I will not let thee go, Un-

til thou bless me, I will not let thee go; Un-

til thou bless me, I will not let thee go.

Wrest - ling Ja - cob, Ja - cob, day is a - break - ing,

Wrest - ling Ja - cob, Ja - cob, I will not let thee go. I'll
(*Or this.*) I'll

hold thee till the break of day, I will not let thee go, Un -
wres - tle till the break of day, I will not let thee go, Un -

D. C.

til thou tell me what's thy name, I will not let thee go.
til thou come and bless my soul, I will not let thee go.

181

There's a love-feast in the heaven by-and-by,

chil-dren, There's a love-feast in the heav-en by-and-

by. Yes, a love-feast in the heav-en by-and-by,

Fine.

chil-dren, There's a love-feast in the heav-en by-and-by.

1. Oh! run up, chil-dren, get your crown, There's a love-feast in the

heav-en by-and-by, And by your Sav-iour's side sit down.

D. S.

There's a love-feast in the heav-en by-and-by. Yes, a

2 Old Satan told me not to pray, &c.
  He wants my soul at the Judgment-day, &c.

3 Oh, brethren, and sisters, how do you do, &c.
  And does your love continue true, &c.

4 Oh, brethren, brethren, how do you know, &c.
  Because my Jesus told me so, &c.

No. 64. When shall I get there.

There's a heaven-ly home up yon-der, There's a heaven-ly home up yon-der, There's a heaven-ly home up yon-der, Oh!

Fine. SOLO.

when shall I get there? 1. Old Pi-late says, I

CHORUS. SOLO.

wash my hands; When shall I get there? I

CHORUS. *D. C.*

find no fault in this just man; When shall I get there?

2 John and Peter ran to see,
    When shall I get there?
But Christ had gone to Galilee,
    When shall I get there?

8 Paul and Silas bound in jail,
    When shall I get there?
They sang and prayed both night and day,
    When shall I get there?

4 I'm bred and born a Methodist,
    When shall I get there?
I carry the witness in my breast,
    When shall I get there!

183

No. 65. There's a Meeting here To-night.

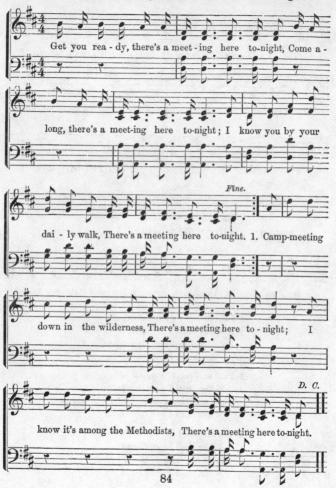

Get you rea - dy, there's a meet - ing here to-night, Come a-

long, there's a meet-ing here to-night; I know you by your

Fine.

dai - ly walk, There's a meeting here to-night. 1. Camp-meeting

down in the wilderness, There's a meeting here to - night; I

D. C.

know it's among the Methodists, There's a meeting here to-night.

2 Those angels wings are tipped with gold, &c.
That brought glad tidings to my soul, &c.

3 My father says it is the best, &c.
To live and die a Methodist, &c.

4 I'm a Methodist bred and a Methodist born, &c.
And when I'm dead there's a Methodist gone, &c.

No. 66.　Farewell, my Brother.

Farewell, my brother,* farewell for-ev - er, Fare you well, my broth-er, now, For I am go-ing home. Oh good-bye, good-bye, For I am bound to leave you, Oh good-bye, good-bye, for I am going home.

After Da Capo sing this:
Shake hands, shake hands, for I am bound to leave you,
Oh, shake hands, &c.

* Or Sister.

Inching along.

[Attention is called to the appropriateness of the melody for the expression of these singular words. It is all embraced within the first three tones of the scale, and thus may be said to be itself not more than an inch long.]

CHORUS.

Keep a inch-ing a - long, Keep a inch-ing a - long;

Je - sus will come by'nd-bye; Keep a inch - ing a - long like a

poor inch-worm, Je-sus will come by'nd-bye. 1. 'Twas a inch by inch I

sought the Lord, Je - sus will come by'nd-bye. And a

inch by inch He blessed my soul, Je - sus will come by'nd-bye.

2 The Lord is coming to take us home,
　Jesus will come by'nd-bye.
And then our work will soon be done,
　Jesus will come by'nd-bye.

3 Trials and troubles are on the way,
　Jesus will come by'nd-bye.
But we must watch and always pray,
　Jesus will come by'nd-bye.

4 We'll inch and inch and inch along,
　Jesus will come by'nd-bye.
And inch and inch till we get home
　Jesus will come by'nd-bye.

186

I ain't got weary yet.

And I ain't got wea-ry yet, And I ain't got wea-ry yet; Been

down in the val-ley so long, And I ain't got wea-ry yet.

SOLO.

CHORUS.

1. Been praying for the sinner so long, And I ain't got wea-ry yet;

DUET.

D. C.

Been praying for the sin-ner so long, And I ain't got wea-ry yet.

2 Been praying for the mourner so long, &c.

3 Been going to the sitting-up so long, &c.

187

No. 69.   Run to Jesus.

[This song was given to the Jubilee Singers by Hon. FREDERICK DOUGLASS, at Washington, D. C., with the interesting statement, that it first suggested to him the thought of escaping from slavery.]

Run to Je - sus, shun the dan - ger, I

don't ex - pect to stay much long - er here. 1. He will

be our dear-est friend, And will help us to the end. I

don't ex-pect to stay much long - er here. Run to Je - sus,

shun the dan - ger, I don't ex-pect to stay much long-er here.

2 Oh, I thought I heard them say,
   There were lions in the way.
     I don't expect, etc.

3 Many mansions there will be,
   One for you and one for me.
     I don't expect, etc.

188

Angels waiting at the Door.

1. My sis-ter's took her flight and gone home, And the
2. She has laid down her cross and gone home, And, &c.
3. She has taken up her crown and gone home, And, &c.

an-gel's wait-ing at the door. My sis-ter's took her

flight and gone home, And the angels waiting at the door.

Tell all my fa-ther's children, Don't you grieve for me;

Tell all my fa-ther's children, Don't you grieve for me.

189

No. 71. Keep your Lamps trimmed.

Keep your lamps trimmed and a-burning, Keep your lamps trimmed and a-

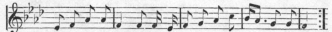

burning, Keep your lamps trimm'd and a-burning, For this work's almost done

Brothers, don't grow wea-ry, Brothers, don't grow wea-ry,
Preachers, &c.

Fine.

Brothers, don't grow wea-ry, For this work's al-most done.

Keep your lamps trimmed and a-burning, Keep your lamps trimmed and a-

burning, Keep your lamps trimm'd and a-burning, For this work's almost done.

'Tis re-lig-ion makes us hap-py, 'Tis re-lig-ion makes us
We are climbing Ja-cob's lad-der, &c.
Ev-ery round goes higher and higher, &c.

hap-py, 'Tis religion, makes us happy, For this work's almost done.

Show Me the Way.

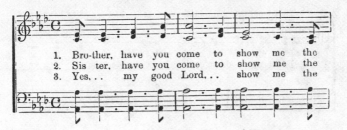

1. Bro-ther, have you come to show me the
2. Sis - ter, have you come to show me the
3. Yes, .. my good Lord, .. show me the

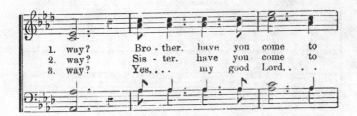

1. way? Bro - ther, have you come to
2. way? Sis - ter, have you come to
3. way? Yes, ... my good Lord, ...

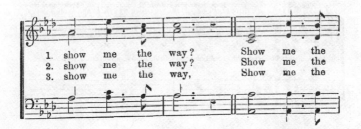

1. show me the way? Show me the
2. show me the way? Show me the
3. show me the way, Show me the

way how to watch and pray.

I've been Redeemed.

Been wash'd in the blood of the Lamb, Been
There is a . . . foun - tain fill'd with blood, Drawn
The dy - ing . . thief re - joic'd to see That

wash'd in the blood of the Lamb, . . . Been
from Im - man - uel's veins; . . . And
foun - tain in his day : . . . . And

wash'd in the blood of the Lamb, . . . That
sin - ners plung'd be - - neath that flood, Lose
there may I, though vile as he, Wash

C.*

flows from Cal - va - ry. . . .
all their guil - ty stains. . .
all my sins a - way. . .

We shall walk thro' the valley and the shadow of death, We shall walk thro' the valley in peace, If Jesus Himself shall be our lead - er, We shall walk thro' the val - ley in peace.

We shall meet those Christians there, meet them there, We shall meet those Chris - tians there, meet them there, If

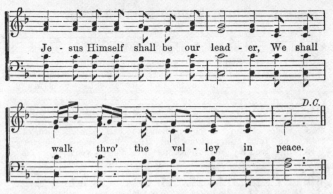

Je - sus Himself shall be our lead - er, We shall

walk thro' the val - ley in peace.

D.C.

2 There will be no sorrow there, If Jesus Himself shall be our leader
There will be no sorrow there, We shall walk thro' the valley in
CHORUS—We shall, &c. [peace

No. 75. Gabriel's Trumpet's going to Blow.

(As sung by Miss JENNIE JACKSON.)

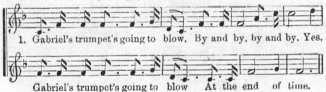

1. Gabriel's trumpet's going to blow, By and by, by and by, Yes,

Gabriel's trumpet's going to blow At the end of time.

2.
Oh, get you all ready for to go
By and by, by and by,
O, get you all ready for to go
At the end of time.

3.
Then my Lord will say to Gabriel,
By and by, by and by, [pet,
Go, get you down your silver trum-
At the end of time.

4.
The first sounding of the trumpet
for the righteous
By and by, by and by,

First sounding of the trumpet for
the righteous,
At the end of time.

5.
Go, wake the sleeping nations,
By and by, by and by,
Go, wake the sleeping nations,
At the end of time.

6.
Then, poor sinner, what will you
By and by, by and by, [do?
You'll run for the mountains to
hide you,
At the end of time.

14 *

Lord, I wish I had a come.

1. Lord, I wish I had a come when you call'd me, Lord, I
2. There's no temp - ta - tions in the heavens, There's
3. My fa - ther and my mo-ther in the heavens, My fa-

1. wish I had a come when you call'd me, Lord, I
2. no tem - ta - tions in the hea - vens, There's
3. -ther and my mo-ther in the hea - vens, My fa-

1. wish I had a come when you call'd me,
2. no temp - ta - tions in the hea - vens,
3. -ther and my mo - ther in the hea - vens,

Sitting by the side of my Je - sus. Way o - ver in the

heavens, Way o - ver in the hea-vens, Way o - ver in the

hea-vens, Sit - ting by the side of my Je - sus.

Deep River.

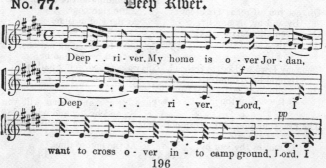

Deep . . ri - ver, My home is o - ver Jor - dan,

Deep . . . . ri - ver, Lord, I

want to cross o - ver in - to camp ground, Lord, I

want to cross o - ver in - to camp ground, Lord, I

pp
want to cross o - ver in - to camp ground, Lord, I

F*ine.*
want to cross o - ver in - to camp ground.

1. Oh, don't you want to go to that Gos-- pel-feast, That
2. I'll go in - to hea - ven, and take my seat,
3. Oh, when I get to heav'n, I'll walk all a - bout, There's

f
1. pro - mis'd land where all is peace? Lord, I
2. Cast my crown at Je - sus' feet. Lord, I
3. nobody there for to turn me out. Lord, I

pp
want to cross o - ver in - to camp ground, Lord, I

f
want to cross o - ver in - to camp ground, Lord, I

pp
want to cross o - ver in - to camp ground, Lord, I

D.C.
want to cross o - ver in - to camp ground.

197

In bright mansions above, In bright mansions above, Lord, I

want to live up yon-der, In bright man-sions a-bove.

1. My father's gone to glory;
2. My brother's gone to glory; } I want to live there too, Lord, I
3. The Christian's gone to glory;

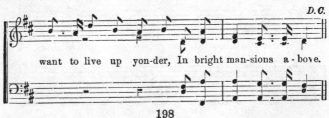

want to live up yon-der, In bright man-sions a-bove.

My Lord, what a Mourning.

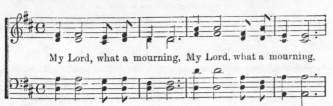

My Lord, what a mourning, My Lord, what a mourning,

My Lord, what a mourning, When the stars begin to fall.
{ 1. You'll
{ 2. You'll
{ 3. You'll

hear the trumpet sound To wake the na-tions un-der ground,
hear the sin-ner mourn, To wake the na-tions un-der ground,
hear the Christian shout, To wake the na-tions un-der ground,

Looking to my God's right hand, When the stars begin to fall.

No. 80. We are climbing the hills of Zion.

(As sung by Miss Jennie Jackson.)

Slowly.

We are climbing the hills of Zi-on, the hills of Zi-on, the

hills of Zi-on, We are climbing the hills of Zi-on,

With Je-sus in our souls.
{ 1. Oh, brethren, do get rea-dy,
{ 2. Oh, seek-er, do get rea-dy,
{ 3. Oh, sin-ner, do get rea-dy,

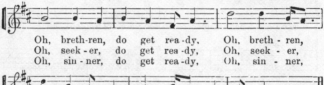

Oh, breth-ren, do get rea-dy, Oh, breth-ren,
Oh, seek-er, do get rea-dy, Oh, seek-er,
Oh, sin-ner, do get rea-dy, Oh, sin-ner,

do get rea-dy, With Je-sus in your souls.

No. 81.   Oh, wasn't that a wide River?

Oh, wasn't that a wide ri-ver, ri-ver of

Jor-dan, Lord? wide ri-ver! There's

200

201

Oh, way over Jordan, View the land, view the land,
Way over Jordan, Oh, view the heav'nly land.
I want to go to heaven when I die! View the land, view the land; To
shout sal-va tion as I fly, Oh, view the heav'n-ly land.

2.

Old Satan's mad, and I am glad,
  View the land, view the land;
He miss'd that soul he thought he
  O view the heav'nly land. [had,
Oh, way over Jordan, &c.

3.

You say you're aiming for the skies,
  View the land, view the land;
Why don't you stop your telling
  O view the heav'nly land. [lies?
Oh, way over Jordan, &c.

4.

You say your Lord has set you free,
  View the land, view the land;
Why don't you let your neighbours be?
  O view the heav'nly land.
Oh, way over Jordan, &c.

We'll overtake the Army.

We'll o - ver-take the ar-my, o - ver-take the ar-my,

FINE.

o - ver - take the ar - my, Yes, my Lord.

1. I've 'list -ed, and I mean to fight; Yes, my Lord, Till
2. Tho' I may fall, I'll bless His name; Yes, my Lord, I'll
3. The God I serve is a man of war; Yes, my Lord, He

D. C.

ev' - ry foe is put to flight, Yes, my Lord
trust in God, and rise a - gain. Yes, my Lord.
fights and con-quers e - ver - more. Yes, my Lord.

We are almost Home.

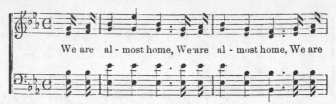

We are al - most home, We are al - most home, We are

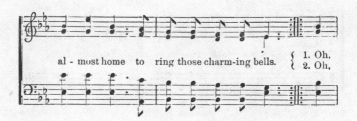

al - most home to ring those charm-ing bells. { 1. Oh,
{ 2. Oh,

come along, brothers, come along, come along, brothers, come along,
come along, sis-ters, come along, come along, sis-ters, come along,

come along, brothers, come along, To ring those charming bells.
come along, sis-ters, come along, To ring those charming bells.

Down by the River.

Oh, we'll wait till Je-sus comes Down by the ri-ver, We'll

FINE.

wait till Je-sus comes Down by the ri - ver side.

{ 1. Oh,
  2. Oh,
  3. Oh,

hal - le - lu - jah to the Lamb, Down by the river; The
we are pil - grims here be - low, Down by the river; Oh,
little did I think that He was so nigh, Down by the river; He

D. C.

Lord is on the giv-ing hand, Down by the ri - ver side.
soon to glo -ry we will go, Down by the ri - ver side.
spake, and made me laugh and cry, Down by the ri - ver side.

Wait a Little While.

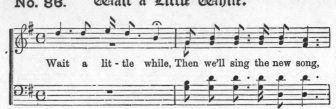

Wait a lit - tle while, Then we'll sing the new song,

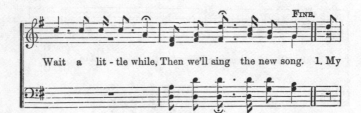

Wait a lit - tle while, Then we'll sing the new song. 1. My

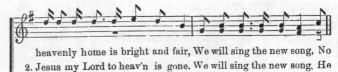

heavenly home is bright and fair, We will sing the new song, No
2. Jesus my Lord to heav'n is gone, We will sing the new song, He

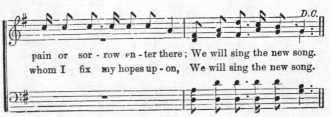

pain or sor - row en - ter there; We will sing the new song.
whom I fix my hopes up - on, We will sing the new song.

Hard Trials.

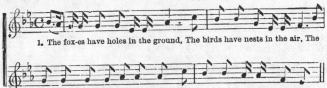

1. The fox-es have holes in the ground, The birds have nests in the air, The Christians have a hiding-place, But we poor sinners have none;

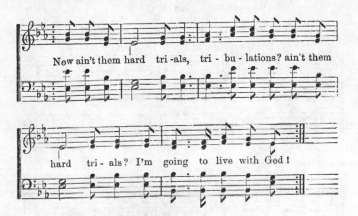

Now ain't them hard tri-als, tri-bu-lations? ain't them hard tri-als? I'm going to live with God!

2 Old Satan tempted Eve,
  And Eve, she tempted Adam;
  And that's why the sinner has to pray so hard
  To get his sins forgiven.

3 Oh, Methodist, Methodist is my name,
  Methodist till I die;
  I'll be baptized on the Methodist side,
  And a Methodist will I die.

4 Oh, Baptist, Baptist is my name,
  Baptist till I die;
  I'll be baptized on the Baptist side,
  And a Baptist will I die,

5 While marching on the road,
  A hunting for a home,
  You had better stop your different
  And travel on to God.

No. 88. He rose from the Dead.

Jews cru-ci-fied Him, and nail'd Him to the tree. The

Jews cru-ci-fied Him, and nail'd Him to the tree, The

Jews cru-ci-fied Him, and nail'd Him to the tree, And the

D.C.

Lord shall bear His chil-dren home.

2 Joseph begged His body, and laid it in the tomb,
And the Lord shall bear His children home.

3 Down came an angel, and rolled the stone away,
And the Lord shall bear His children home.

4 Mary, she came weeping, her Lord for to see,
But Christ had gone to Galilee.

15

Swing low, sweet cha - ri - ot, Swing low, sweet cha - ri - ot,

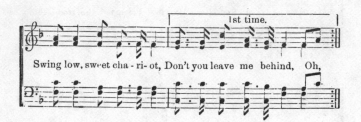

Swing low, sweet cha - ri- ot, Don't you leave me behind, Oh,

rit. 2nd time. **FINE.**

Don't you leave me behind.

1. Good old chariot, swing so low,
2. Good old chariot, take us all home,

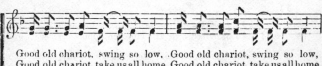

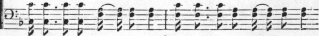

Good old chariot, swing so low, Good old chariot, swing so low,
Good old chariot, take us all home, Good old chariot, take us all home,

210

D.C.

Don't you leave me be-hind. Oh,

No. 90.   Grace.

The following " Grace before Meat " is printed at the request of numerous friends of the Jubilee Singers.

Arr. from P. P. BLISS.

Thou art great, and Thou art good, And we thank Thee

for this food; By Thy hand must all be fed,

Give us, Lord, our dai - ly bread. A - men.

15 *

No. 91. **Oh yes! Oh yes!**

2 As I went down in the valley to pray, Oh yes !
I met old Satan on the way, Oh yes !
And what do you think he said to me, Oh yes !
"You're too young to pray, and too young to die," Oh yes !

3 If you want to catch that heavenly breeze, Oh yes !
Go down in the valley on your knees, Oh yes !
Go, bow your knees upon the ground, Oh yes ! ·
And ask your Lord to turn you round, Oh yes !

A Happy New Year.

What a hap-py new year, What a hap-py new year, What a

FINE.

hap-py, what a hap-py, what a hap-py new year.

1. I'm run-ning thro' grace To that hap-py place; Thro'

D.C.

grace I'm de-ter-min'd To see my Lord's face.

2.
One thing I do find,
I'll keep it in mind,
He won't live in glory
And leave me behind.

3.
O sinner, believe
Christ will you receive,
For all things are ready,
And you stand in need.

'Tis Jordan's River.

'Tis Jor-dan's ri - ver, and I must go 'cross, 'Tis

Jor-dan's ri - ver, and I must go 'cross, 'Tis

Jor-dan's ri - ver, and I must go 'cross; Poor

sin-ner, fare you well. 1. Am I a sol-dier of the Cross?

D.C.

Yes, my Lord! Or must I count this soul as lost? Yes, my Lord

2 As I go down the stream of time, Yes. my Lord :
  I leave this sinful world behind, Yes, my Lord!

3 Old Satan thinks he'll get us all, Yes, my Lord!
  Because in Adam we did fall, Yes, my Lord!

4 If you want to see old Satan run, Yes, my Lord!
  Just shoot him with a Gospel-gun, Yes, my Lord!

No. 94.   Good-bye, Brothers.

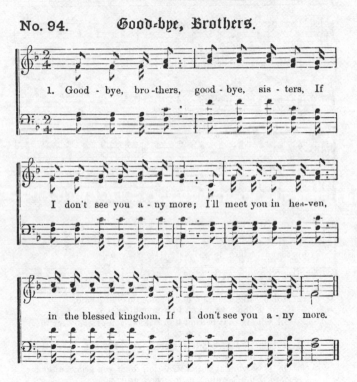

1. Good - bye, bro-thers, good - bye, sis - ters, If
I don't see you a - ny more; I'll meet you in hea-ven,
in the blessed kingdom, If I don't see you a - ny more.

2 We'll part in the body, we'll meet in the spirit,
  If I don't see you any more;
  So now God bless you, God bless you,
  If I don't see you any more.
      Then good-bye, brothers, &c.

215

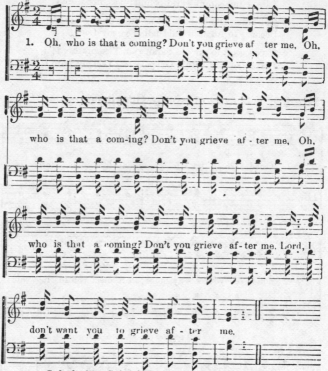

1. Oh, who is that a coming? Don't you grieve af ter me, Oh,
who is that a com-ing? Don't you grieve af-ter me, Oh,
who is that a coming? Don't you grieve af-ter me. Lord, I
don't want you to grieve af - ter me.

2 It looks like Gabriel, don't you grieve after me,
  Lord, I don't want you to grieve after me.

3 Oh, who is that behind him? don't you grieve after me,
  Lord, I don't want you to grieve after me.

4 It looks like Jesus, don't you grieve after me,
  Lord, I don't want you to grieve after me.

5 Go, blow your trumpet, Gabriel, don't you grieve after me,
  Lord, I don't want you to grieve after me.

6 How loud must I blow it? don't you grieve after me,
  Lord, I don't want you to grieve after me.

7 Loud as seven claps of thunder! don't you grieve after me,
  Lord, I don't want you to grieve after me.

8 To wake the sleeping nations, don't you grieve after me,
  Lord, I don't want you to grieve after me.

Rise and Shine.

Oh, brethren, rise and shine, and give God the glo-ry, glo-ry,

Then you must rise, &c.

Rise and shine, and give God the glo - ry, glo - ry.

FINE.

Rise and shine, and give God the glory, for the year of Ju - bi - lee.

1. Don't you want to be a sol-dier, sol-dier, sol-dier, Don't you

want to be a sol-dier, sol-dier, sol-dier? Don't you

want to be a sol-dier, sol-dier, sol-dier for the

year of Ju - bi - lee?

2 Do you think I will make a soldier,
For the year of Jubilee?

3 Yes, I think you will make a soldier,
For the year of Jubilee!

*Sing the three verses in succession, and after the third verse go back to the
beginning, and sing the words, " Then you must rise," &c.*

No. 97. Now we take this Feeble Body.

This hymn is much used at funerals, and especially while bearing the body and lowering it into the grave.

1. Now we take this fee - ble bo - dy, And we
2. Now we take this dear old fa - ther, And we
3. Now we lift our mourn - ful voi - ces, As we

car - ry it to the grave, And we all leave it there, Hal - le-
car - ry him to the grave, And we all leave him there, Hal lo-
gather around the grave, And we weep as we sing, Hal - le-

lu - jah, And a Hal-le - lu - jah, and a Hal-le - lu - jah, And we
lu - jah, And a Hal-le - lu - jah, and a Hal-le - lu - jah, And we
lu - jah, And a Hal-le - lu - jah, and a Hal-le - lu - jah, And we

all leave it there, Halle-lu-jah, And a Hal-le - lu-jah, and a Hal-le-
all leave him there, Hallelujah, And a Hal-le - lu - jah, and a Hal-le-
weep as we sing, Halle-lu - jah. And a Hal-le - lu - jah, and a Hal-le-

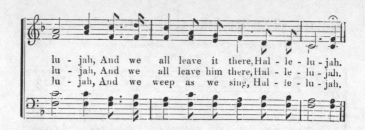

lu - jah, And we all leave it there, Hal - le - lu - jah.
lu - jah, And we all leave him there, Hal - le - lu - jah.
lu - jah, And we weep as we sing, Hal - le - lu - jah.

No. 98. Shine, Shine.

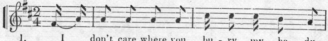

1. I don't care where you bu - ry my bo - dy,
2. You may bu - ry my bo - dy in the Egypt garden,
3. I'm go - ing to join the forty-four thou - sand,
4. Great big stars way up yonder,

Don't care where you bu - ry my bo - dy, Don't care where you
Bury my body in the Egypt garden, Bury my body in
Going to join the forty - four thousand, Going to join the
Great big stars way up yonder, Great big stars

bu - ry my bo - dy,
the Egypt garden,
forty - four thousand, } O my lit-tle soul's going to shine, shine,
way up yonder,

O my little soul's going to shine, shine, All around the heaven going to

shine, shine, All a - round the heaven going to shine, shine.

220

Anchor in the Lord.

Anchor, be-liev-er, anchor, an-chor in the Lord,

FINE

Throw your anchor any way, an-chor in the Lord

1. Throw it to my dear mother's door,
2. Throw it to my dear father's door, } An-chor in the Lord.
3. Throw it to my dear sister's door,

Throw it to my dear mother's door, }
Throw it to my dear father's door, } An-chor in the Lord.
Throw it to my dear sister's door,

221

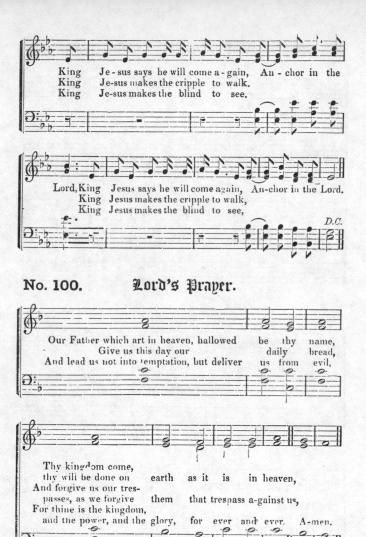

King   Je - sus says he will come a - gain,   An - chor in the
King   Je-sus makes the cripple to walk.
King   Je-sus makes the blind to see.

Lord, King   Jesus says he will come again,   An-chor in the Lord.
King   Jesus makes the cripple to walk,
King   Jesus makes the blind to see,

D.C.

No. 100. Lord's Prayer.

Our Father which art in heaven, hallowed   be   thy   name,
Give us this day our   daily   bread,
And lead us not into temptation, but deliver   us from evil,

Thy kingdom come,
thy will be done on   earth as it is in heaven,
And forgive us our tres-
passes, as we forgive them that trespass a-gainst us,
For thine is the kingdom,
and the power, and the glory, for ever and ever. A-men.

No. 101. John Brown's Body.

Sing the verses in the order in which they are numbered. Do not sing the chorus after the third verse, but go at once to the fourth, and then close with the chorus.

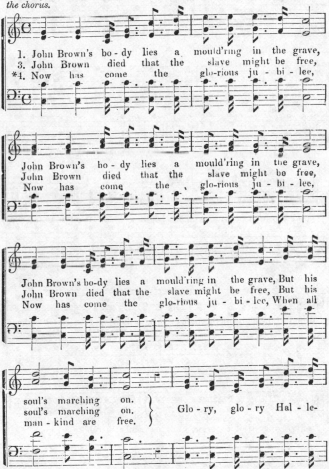

1. John Brown's bo-dy lies a mould'ring in the grave,
3. John Brown died that the slave might be free,
*4. Now has come the glo-rious ju-bi-lee,

John Brown's bo-dy lies a mould'ring in the grave,
John Brown died that the slave might be free,
Now has come the glo-rious ju-bi-lee,

John Brown's bo-dy lies a mould'ring in the grave, But his
John Brown died that the slave might be free, But his
Now has come the glo-rious ju-bi-lee, When all

soul's marching on.
soul's marching on. } Glo-ry, glo-ry Hal-le-
man-kind are free.

* The words of the fourth verse do not correspond fully to the notes, but the adaptation can be easily made by the singer.

223

lu-jah, Glo-ry, glo-ry Hal-le - lu-jah, Glo - ry, glo-ry Hal-le-

lujah, His soul's marching on. 2. He captured Harper's Ferry with his

nineteen men so true, And he frightened old Vir-gi - nia till she

trembled through and through. They hung him for a traitor, them-

selves the traitor crew, But his soul's marching on.

Listen to the Angels.

Where do you think I found my soul, Listen to the angels shouting, I found my soul at hell's dark door, Listen to the angels shouting, Be-fore I lay in hell one day, Listen to the angels shouting, I sing and pray my soul a-way, Listen to the angels shouting.

Run all the way, run all the way, Run all the way my Lord, Listen to the angels shouting. Blow, Gabriel, blow, Blow, Gabriel, blow, Tell all the joyful news, Listen to the angels shouting. I don't know what sinner want to stay here for, Listen to the angels shouting. When he gets home he will sor-row no more, Listen to the angels shouting. Run all the way, etc.

Brethren, will you come to the promised land, *See arch, etc.*
Come all and sing with the heavenly band, *See arch, etc.*

Let us move along, move along, move along to the
heavenly home, Let us move along, move along I am
bound to meet you there.

FINE.

{ 1. We are on the ocean
{ 2. Yon-der see the golden
{ 3. There we'll meet our friends in

sailing, And a - while must face the stormy blast, But if
city, And the light-house gleaming on the shore, Hear the
Jesus, Who are wait - ing on the golden shore, With a

D.C.

Jesus is our captain, We will make the port at last.
angels sweetly singing, Soon our journey will be o'er.
shout of joy they'll greet us, When we meet to part no more.

No. 104. The Angels changed my Name.

1. I went to the hill side, I went to pray, I
2. I looked at my hands and my hands were new, I

know the an - gels done changed my name, Done
know the an - gels done changed my name, I

changed my name for the com - ing day, Thank
looked at my feet and my feet were too, Thank

CHORUS.

God the angels done changed my name. } Done
God the angels done changed my name. }

changed my name for the coming day, I know the angels done

changed my name, Done changed my name for the

coming day, Thank God the angels done changed my name.

227   16 *

Bright Sparkles in the Churchyard.

As Sung by the "Hampton Students."

May the Lord, He will be glad of me, May the Lord, He will be glad of me, May the Lord, He will be glad of me, . . . In the heaven He'll re-joice. In the heaven once, In the hea-ven twice, In the hea-ven He'll re-joice. In the heaven once, In the heaven twice, In the heaven He'll rejoice.

Duo—*Soprano and Tenor.*

Bright spar-kles in the churchyard Give light un-to the tomb,

Trio—*1st and 2nd Soprano and Alto.*

Bright summer, Spring's o - ver, Sweet flow-ers in their bloom.

Quartette.

Bright spar-kles in the churchyard Give light un - to the

tomb, Bright summer, Spring's o-ver, Sweet flowers in their bloom.

Tutti.

My mo-ther once, my mo-ther twice, my mo-ther, she'll re -

229

-joice; In the hea-ven, once, in the hea-ven, twice, In the

time. | 2nd time.

hea-ven she'll re-joice, In the hea-ven she'll re-joice.

p

Mother, rock me in the cra-dle all the day, . . . Mother, all the day,

rock me in the cra-dle all the day, . . . Mo-ther,

rock me in the cra-dle all the day, . . . Mo-ther, all the day,

230

rock me in the cra-dle all the day,

QUARTETTE.

All the day, . . . all the day, . . . Oh,
all the day, all the day,

rock me in the cra-dle all the day, . . . all the day, all the

day, all the day, Oh, rock me in the
all the day,

cra-dle all the day. Oh, mother, don't you love your darling

231

child, Oh, rock me in the cra-dle all the day.... day.

Mo-ther, rock me in the cra-dle, Mother, rock me in the

cra-dle, Mother, rock me in the cra -dle all the day, . . .

Mo-ther, day, All the day, . . . all the day, . . .
all the day, all the
. . . Oh, rock me in the cra - dle, all the day, . . .
day,

all the day,   all the day, Oh,

all the day, . . .   all the day, . . .

rock me in the cra - dle all the   day.   You may

lay me down to sleep, my mother dear, Oh, rock me in the cradle all the

day, . . .   You may lay me down to sleep, my mother   dear,

Dim - in - u - en - do.

. . . Oh, rock me in the cra - dle all the day. . . . . .

all the day.

233

Come down, Angels.

CHORUS.

Come down, angels, trouble the water, Come down, angels, trouble the water,

1st time.

Come down, angels, trouble the water, Let God's saints come in, Oh,

2nd time. FINE.

Let God's saints come in.

1. I love to shout, I love to sing, Let God's
2. I think I hear the sinner say, Let God's
3. I hope to meet my brother there, Let God's
4. Didn't Jesus tell you once before, Let God's

D.C.

saints come in, I love to praise my heav'nly King, Let God's saints come in.
saints come in, My Saviour taught me how to pray, Let God's saints come in.
saints come in, That us'd to join with me in pray'r, Let God's saints come in.
saints come in, To go in peace and sin no more, Let God's saints come in.

234

I'm so Glad.

I'm so glad the angels brought the tidings down, I'm so glad, I'm

hunt-ing for a home, Oh, hunting for a home.

1. You'll
2. Oh,
3. A
4. Tho

1. not get lost in the wil-der-ness, Hunting for a home, With the
2. Chris-tians, you had better pray, Hunting for a home, For
3. lit - tle long - er here be - low, Hunting for a home, And
4. an - gels sang in Beth-le-hem, Hunting for a home,

1. love of Je - sus in your breast, Hunting for a home. . .
2. Sa-tan's round you ev'-ry day, Hunting for a home.
3. then to glo - ry we will go, Hunting for a home.
4. Peace on earth, good-will to men, Hunting for a home.

No. 108. Peter, go Ring them Bells.

1. Oh, Peter, go ring them bells, Peter, go ring them bells, Peter, go

To Chorus after D.C.

ring them bells, I heard from heaven to-day. I wonder where my

mo-ther is gone, I won-der where my mo-ther is gone, I

D.C.

wonder where my mother is gone, I heard from heaven to-day.

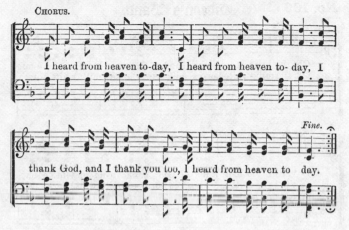

CHORUS.

I heard from heaven to-day, I heard from heaven to-day, I
thank God, and I thank you too, I heard from heaven to day.

Fine.

2.

I wonder where sister Mary's gone—
    I heard from heaven to-day;
I wonder where sister Martha's gone—
    I heard from heaven to-day;
It's good news, and I thank God—
    I heard from heaven to-day;
Oh, Peter, go ring them bells—
    I heard from heaven to-day.

      CHORUS.—I heard from heaven, &c.

3.

I wonder where brother Moses gone—
    I heard from heaven to-day;
I wonder where brother Daniel's gone—
    I heard from heaven to-day;
He's gone where Elijah has gone
    I heard from heaven to-day;
Oh, Peter, go ring them bells—
    I heard from heaven to-day.

      CHORUS.—I heard from heaven, &c.

237

Oh, the band of Gid-e-on, band of Gid-e-on, band of Gid-e-on,
Oh, the milk-white horses, milk-white horses, milk-white horses,

o - ver in Jor-dan, Band of Gid - e -on, band of Gid - e -on,
o - ver in Jor-dan, Milk-white hors - es, milk-white hors - es,

DUET.

How I long to see that day. 1. I hail to my sis-ter, my

sis-ter she bow low, Say, don't you want to go to hea - ven?

CHORUS.

How I long to see that day. { Oh, the twelve white hors-es,
{ Oh, hitch 'em to the chariot,

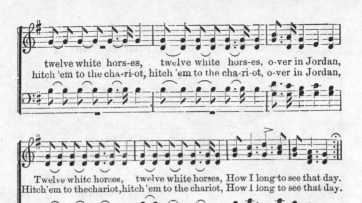

twelve white hors-es,   twelve white hors-es, o-ver in Jordan,
hitch 'em to the cha-ri-ot, hitch 'em to the cha-ri-ot, o-ver in Jordan,

Twelve white horses,   twelve white horses, How I long to see that day.
Hitch 'em to thechariot, hitch 'em to the chariot, How I long to see that day.

DUET.—I hail to my brother, my brother he bow low,
     Say, don't you want to go to heaven?
     How I long to see that day !
CHORUS.—Oh, ride up in the chariot, ride up in the chariot,
     Ride up in the chariot over in Jordan ;
     Ride up in the chariot, ride up in the chariot,
     How I long to see that day !
     It's a golden chariot, a golden chariot,
     Golden chariot over in Jordan ;
     Golden chariot, a golden chariot—
     How I *long* to see that day !

DUET.—I hail to the mourner, the mourner he bow low,
     Say, don't you want to go to heaven?
     How I long to see that day !
CHORUS.—Oh, the milk and honey, milk and honey,
     Milk and honey over in Jordan ;
     Milk and honey, milk and honey—
     How I long to see that day !
     Oh, the healing water, the healing water,
     Healing water over in Jordan ;
     Healing water, the healing water—
     How I *long* to see that day !

In that Great Getting=up Morning.

As Sung by the "Hampton Students."

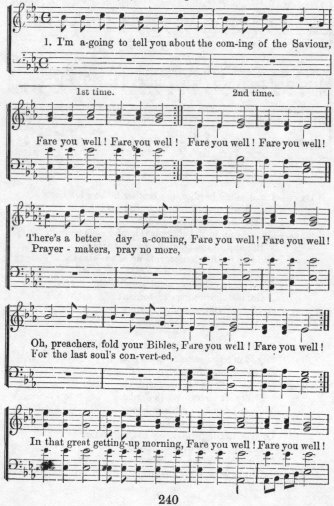

1. I'm a-going to tell you about the com-ing of the Saviour,

1st time.   2nd time.

Fare you well! Fare you well!   Fare you well! Fare you well!

There's a better   day a-coming, Fare you well! Fare you well!
Prayer - makers, pray no more,

Oh, preachers, fold your Bibles, Fare you well! Fare you well!
For the last soul's con-vert-ed,

In that great getting-up morning, Fare you well! Fare you well!

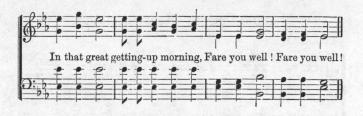

In that great getting-up morning, Fare you well ! Fare you well !

2.

The Lord spoke to Gabriel:
Go look behind the altar,
Take down the silver trumpet,
Blow your trumpet, Gabriel.
Lord, how loud shall I blow it?
Blow it right calm and easy,
Do not alarm My people,
Tell them to come to judgment;
Gabriel, blow your trumpet.
Lord, how loud shall I blow it?
Loud as seven peals of thunder!
Wake the sleeping nations.

3.

Then you'll see poor sinners rising;
Then you'll see the world on fire;
See the moon a-bleeding,
See the stars falling,
See the elements melting,
See the forkèd lightning,
Hear the rumbling thunder;
Earth shall reel and totter.
Then you'll see the Christians rising;
Then you'll see the righteous marching,
See them marching home to heaven.
Then you'll see my Jesus coming
With all His holy angels,
Take the righteous home to heaven,
There they'll live with God for ever.

I know that my Redeemer lives.

Oh, I know, I know, my Lord, I know, and I

know that my Redeemer lives.

Just stand right still, & steady yourself, I
Oh, Da-niel in the li-on's den, I
Oh, Caleb and Joshua, the very ones, I
Just watch that sun, and see how it runs, I

know that my Re-deemer lives.

Oh, just let me tell you about the
Oh, none but Je-sus is
That prayed to God for to
Oh, don't let it catch you with
your

D. C.

God Him-self,
Daniel's friend,
stop the sun,
work undone,

I know that my Re-deem-er lives.

Sweet Canaan.

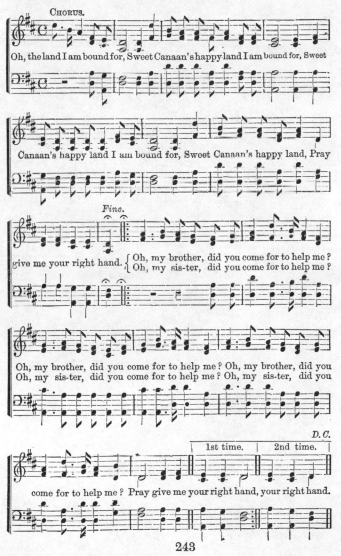

CHORUS.

Oh, the land I am bound for, Sweet Canaan's happy land I am bound for, Sweet
Canaan's happy land I am bound for, Sweet Canaan's happy land, Pray

Fine.

give me your right hand. { Oh, my brother, did you come for to help me ?
{ Oh, my sis-ter, did you come for to help me ?

Oh, my brother, did you come for to help me ? Oh, my brother, did you
Oh, my sis-ter, did you come for to help me ? Oh, my sis-ter, did you

D. C.

1st time. | 2nd time.

come for to help me ? Pray give me your right hand, your right hand.

243